The Prepper Preparedness Guide

Long Term Backyard Survival

Ron Foster

Alabama, USA

ISBN-13:
978-1978102026

ISBN-10:
197810202X

Printed in the United States of America

Preface

So you want to be able to survive in your backyard? Well that is what I am about to tell you about but keep in mind it doesn't replace well planned disaster preps that I hope you will continue to stockpile. However this book will prepare you to as I am often heard to say "Lose everything but your mind" and survive.

It is a very smart move on your part to want to shelter in place or "Bug In" as it were. Maybe you already consider yourself a seasoned prepper and just want some more knowledge, could be you are a novice to the preparedness community and need a place to start gaining some real solid food procurement knowledge and skills, I plan on entertaining and accommodating you both with this book so bear with me as I address both concerns.

The main thing in your favor is that you have chosen to take the big step toward avoiding a potentially suicidal bugging out scenario and having the good sense to stay at home to take care of yourself and your family and for this I commend you.

I sincerely hope you are benefited and pleased by the real life practical knowledge that I hope you will learn in this book. This is because I am a bit of a rarity out here, I am what you call a "Prepper's Prepper." This title I wear is not one I bestowed on myself, but one bestowed on me by my peers and its hard won let me tell you.

I know there are many so called survival experts out here touting their expertise, blogs, books and wares but you see I have seen it, done it, been there so long I have learned what truly matters in this life of being preparedness minded and disaster ready. I have come to the final conclusion that only one thing matters to me and that is getting the preparedness message out so that I will enough community members around to help rebuild society.

I want to take a moment to explain why I wrote this book. Not for the money, although I am a bit of a mercenary and have for many years lived the lifestyle of supporting my prepper lifestyle in this manner of publishing as a prolific prepper fiction author. Not for the praise, I already know I know my bush craft and preparedness stuff and although some Amazon rating stars and a pat on the back once in awhile is nice , I am not here to prove anything. I am here to teach you how to have a chance at surviving with some degree of confidence these apocalyptic times we are challenged with and show you how to do it on a very tight budget.

As for me undertaking to write this book as a journalistic adventure, well my readers already know I have applied my talents and imagination to

Preface

So you want to be able to survive in your backyard? Well that is what I am about to tell you about but keep in mind it doesn't replace well planned disaster preps that I hope you will continue to stockpile. However this book will prepare you to as I am often heard to say "Lose everything but your mind" and survive.

It is a very smart move on your part to want to shelter in place or "Bug In" as it were. Maybe you already consider yourself a seasoned prepper and just want some more knowledge, could be you are a novice to the preparedness community and need a place to start gaining some real solid food procurement knowledge and skills, I plan on entertaining and accommodating you both with this book so bear with me as I address both concerns.

The main thing in your favor is that you have chosen to take the big step toward avoiding a potentially suicidal bugging out scenario and having the good sense to stay at home to take care of yourself and your family and for this I commend you.

I sincerely hope you are benefited and pleased by the real life practical knowledge that I hope you will learn in this book. This is because I am a bit of a rarity out here, I am what you call a "Prepper's Prepper." This title I wear is not one I bestowed on myself, but one bestowed on me by my peers and its hard won let me tell you.

I know there are many so called survival experts out here touting their expertise, blogs, books and wares but you see I have seen it, done it, been there so long I have learned what truly matters in this life of being preparedness minded and disaster ready. I have come to the final conclusion that only one thing matters to me and that is getting the preparedness message out so that I will enough community members around to help rebuild society.

I want to take a moment to explain why I wrote this book. Not for the money, although I am a bit of a mercenary and have for many years lived the lifestyle of supporting my prepper lifestyle in this manner of publishing as a prolific prepper fiction author. Not for the praise, I already know I know my bush craft and preparedness stuff and although some Amazon rating stars and a pat on the back once in awhile is nice , I am not here to prove anything. I am here to teach you how to have a chance at surviving with some degree of confidence these apocalyptic times we are challenged with and show you how to do it on a very tight budget.

As for me undertaking to write this book as a journalistic adventure, well my readers already know I have applied my talents and imagination to that task prodigiously in over 50 fiction books already on the subject and have a love for quirky characters getting along and surviving apocalyptic worlds while teaching all sorts of hunting fishing, trapping, bartering tips and tricks.

My internet trolls or non southern speaking literary detractors know my editing isn't always up to snuff but most of my readers are kind enough to overlook a lot of my efforts because I do deliver a good story along with a LOT of survival tips and tricks they didn't know, but it's not about that... It is about me actually sitting down here and teaching you how to survive my way and putting some simple hard living down and dirty techniques on paper that require little effort (think not calorie burning physical exercise) that will hopefully keep you from having to wander around and be exposed to other desperate survivors that might challenge or harm you.

In that considerable library of mine that I have created over the years, I hope many of you have noticed that my characters and particularly the heroes I write about that try to guide survivor reconstruction communities have never had to actually shoot anyone.

Now if you want a book about blood and gore or how to be a ninja or Navy Seal gung ho soldier go read someone's zombie apocalypse genre. Now if you want to learn how to not shoot anyone or get shot in a grid down situation keep reading my writings and notice also I don't usually repeat a survival tip or trick in all those many books.

Oh, I can be as nasty of a adversary as they come, I have the training and mindset for it but I am getting to be a old man and sort of have learned enough sometimes painful life lessons the hard way to already know you don't dwell on the dark side of human nature if you truly want to survive,

True survival in my opinion is all about community and being a productive and knowdgeble member of the social order that attempts to benefit themselves and others. A person that can make a difference to the community in some small way to help solve problems and lead others in times of disaster as well as try to avoid the general social unrest in a peaceful manner. This is why I chose disaster preparedness as my life's work and decided to get advanced degrees in Emergency Management and advocate for state and federal holistic response versus the popular military model that wants to herd everyone into a shelter and disarm them. About the best thing I learned was that the government does not have a plan for a nationwide disaster unless you count the Army and continuity of government.

I no longer engage in public or administrator position policy advocacy for this holistic model of creating disaster resistant and self-sufficient resilient communities.

I instead focus my energies along with a great deal of time on my own public preparedness social media warnings and published fiction and nonfiction manuscripts regarding wisdom sharing with the prepper community so that individuals can take care of themselves as best they can no matter what their financial capabilities may be.

In conclusion, please remember the old prepper adage about "the more knowledge we know the less we need to carry to survive."

Acknowledgements

Patricia Lambert
My sometimes editor, my lover
my friend and prepper soulmate

Contents

Contents

GETTING STARTED WITH THE BASICS

Let's face it; the majority of us won't be bugging out should a mega disaster strike unless we are forced to. The first thing to consider in becoming a prepper is avoiding costly mistakes. The term 'Bugging Out' refers to the decision to abandon your home due to an unexpected emergency situation–whether a natural disaster or one caused by man. Most preppers at first become fascinated with reading about the concept and the gear in the blogs and forums about Bug out Bags and devote a lot of time, energy and money creating what they consider is the ultimate one for themselves.

So why are we talking about bugging out when this book is supposed to be about sheltering in place or bugging in? Because you most likely already have plenty of "stuff" to help you survive and I don't want you to buy one dang thing more gear wise and start a "bug in" bag. Consider your bug out bag as dual use from here on out. You already got what you need most likely. Anything else that I suggest to you I bet you already have in your household or can accumulate very cheaply.

This kit is also referred to as a 72-Hour Bag, a Get Out Of Dodge Bag, not to be confused with a get home bag which generally has less items and is designed to get you from your workplace to your house should you have to walk. The thought of having to evacuate your home due to a sudden and imminent threat is not at all unrealistic. The reality is that sudden and uncontrollable events of nature and man do happen. Bug out bags definitely have their place, leave yours packed and consider that kitchen drawer you have containing odd bits of this and that like string, old empty Bic lighters and picture wire your bug in box.

Now a bug out bag or BOB is only supposed to contain the gear that one would need to survive for 72 hours if evacuating from a disaster but somewhere along the way it seems people start designing them to last even longer and make some kind of long term survival kit out of it with all kinds of giz whizzs.

This is usually when things get out of hand and they end up with so much gear they couldn't possibly carry it in a backpack and get delusional notions about bugging out to the woods. Don't think you should pack your bug out bag with as many items as possible. In fact, I think you should check your bag for any non-essential items with a large weight-to-space ratio and remove them. Ideally, a bug out bag should weigh about 15% of your body weight, assuming you're in decent shape. 20% of your body weight should be the absolute maximum. Let me go on record here and state that for most people bugging out to some remote woods is a suicide mission. It takes a great deal of knowledge and woodsman experience to even attempt to try to live off the land and even then chances are high you might not make it. Game will be scarce and tons of inexperienced hunters will fill the woods. You're much better off bugging in, being safe and riding a disaster out living off your food storage. Take all that gear you pulled out of your backpack to lighten your load and put it in a catch all surplus bag.

If you are bound and determined to bug out to the woods someday or you think you might be forced to, I suggest you look at a book I published back in 2003 called the THE RURAL RANGER A SUBURBAN AND URBAN SURVIVAL MANUAL & FIELD GUIDE OF TRAPS AND SNARES FOR FOOD AND SURVIVAL I will touch on wild game procurement in this book enough that you will be proficient in a backyard but it's not what this guide is all about.

You also might be surprised to know that in many areas there is more wild game living in the city than the adjoining forest lands. The answer to why this is a fact that can be answered relatively simply, basically it's simply because the city offers the animals' easier food and shelter than the woods does. They are like us, lazy and adaptable modern conveniences.

If you are bugging in, that is you are definitely staying in your home which should be your focus by the way, you need to work on what's called backyard survival if you're thinking long-term grid down staying at home.

Don't let the prepping bug bite you again and cause your own economic collapse doing so. If you have been buying a little extra food every month to put back for an emergency, don't change a thing or add unnecessary extra expense making over your backyard.

If you are going to pursue gardening more extensively or permaculture landscape your yard after reading this book, that's on you and your budget but start small and learn what works in your own growing zone and soil conditions before investing too much or buying the wrong thing.

Meantime let's assume you are not going to do anything with your back lawn at all other than mow it and maintain it all the way up to the dreaded day a Solar storm, EMP, hackers, terrorists or some other kind of disaster takes the electrical grid down. I am going to suggest some supplies for you to purchase that can dramatically increase your chances of success but these can be purchased 5 Orc $10 at a time and cap out the complete system for around $50 max. I will also tell you how to arrive at a location or walk out your backdoor with nothing but your hands in your pockets to do the same thing but your results will suffer and surviving will be more difficult for you.

2

IMPROVING THE ODDS

Your backyard is a microcosm, one that is suitable for many forms of interdependent life. It would be wonderful if everyone had as a "Bug In Backyard" some kind of picturesque wilderness meadow right outside their kitchen window but for most of us poor preppers out here this is highly unlikely.

We might not have that much land but we can benefit by borrowing personalized elements of this mythical meadow that we would like to perceive into our own backyards. We can select or add edible plants and herbs to attract beneficial insects, song birds and other wild creatures we would like present. We can add medicinal plants or make hedges.

Perhaps you don't want a wild meadow right now and prefer a manicured lawn or your home owners association limits the type of landscaping you can do. Could be that you simply don't have the time, money or energy to invest in upgrading your close proximity environment to anything more than a grass lawn. All these situations are workable and survivable however

Oh yea I admit its harder to survive in the desert than on a seashore but its still doable and lot of the survival skills you need for both are interchangeable, this applies to backyards also.

First off let's look at your own personal backyard view as a young boy or girl would do when considering pitching a tent and having a sleep over. What places appear to be the most likely spots to make a camp or build a fort at?

I bet your kids if you have any could tell you which spots are better and why than you can. That is because they have probably spent more time back there than you. They know the low spots on the ground where the rain gathers, which spots seem to be buggier or mosquito prone etc.

Look at your backyard with youthful eyes for the first time that you have in a longtime and remember your childhood. What possibilities do you see? What secrets does your land hold? Go investigate, be curious and observe and imagine!

What is it that you want to prioritize now? Perhaps find an area and start a small garden to grow your own food? Cultivate your gardening skills now before you're life depends on your green thumb is a big step in the right direction.

Are you considering adding a barbeque grill or fire pit? This would also make a great place for practicing your fire making skills or figuring out or teaching about fire steel before the poo hits the fan.

Every backyard lawn has weeds. Learning to *safely* identify wild edibles for nutrition and medicine is smart. Like every other skill mentioned above, wild crafting can be done close to home. There are many resources available to help you identify wild edibles.

Fortification And Security

Before you start edible landscaping your yard please pause to consider also adding to your security with a few well placed plants.

Out west the pioneers used to build fences of cactus to guard from Indian attack. Now I am not suggesting anything that radical but a good edible prickly pear or Hawthorne hedge deters folks nicely.

HAWTHORNE HIDEAWAY

Hawthorn is a common hedgerow tree, often planted to create an impenetrable barrier for live stock. As the name suggests, it is covered in thorns, Hawthorn trees (Crataegus spp.) are commonly planted in rows as hedges in U.S. Department of Agriculture plant hardiness zones 4 through 8. The trees are highly adaptable, able to flourish in many different soil conditions.

The Hawthorn (Crataegus mongyna), Whitethorn, Haegthorn, Quickthorn) The Hawthorn's many names reflect its uses and properties; Haegthorn is Anglo-Saxon and refers to its use as a hedging plant, and Quickthorn referring to the live hedge or boundary formed by living plants of Hawthorn. Another name for the Hawthorn is the "Bread and Cheese Tree". This refers to the young leaves and leaf buds which country folk would eat straight from the tree. They have a sweet nutty flavor and can be added to salads along with the flower buds. A liquor was made from hawthorn buds and brandy. Formerly the timber, when of sufficient size, was used for making small articles, for handles, and because of its hardness, for engravers' blocks. The root wood was used for making boxes and combs. The wood has a fine grain and polishes up beautifully. It was most desirable as a fuel wood as it burns very hot

LEAVES – the name 'bread and cheese' is referring to the leaves which have a nutty and pleasant taste, as long as they are very young when eaten.

BERRIES – Late in the year you will notice lots of red berries appear on the hawthorn. These berries are known as 'haws'. Birds will feed on these through the winter, and so can we, although they don't really taste very much, and are dominated by a stone, which must not be cracked so be sure to spit it out! The stone is often made up of several segments which tend to fuse together to appear as one. The berries are mostly used to make jams, and fruit leathers. The red berries (haws) are a significant food source for birds.

SEEDS – the seeds should not be cracked when eating the flesh of the berry, but they can be roasted and ground into a coffee substitute.

Hawthorn has throughout history been used to treat kidney and bladder problems.

In the 19th century hawthorn was recognized as an excellent heart remedy. This herb is non-toxic.

Hawthorn is probably the best natural heart remedy known to us.

The haws (red berries) do wonders for the functions of the heart. Hawthorn is packed with protective actions on the heart.

The blood flows more freely through the blood vessels and this increases the amount of blood pumped by the heart.

Hawthorn is used to treat irregular heartbeat, angina and heart failure.

As hawthorn increases blood circulation, it is good for people who get the feeling of inching needles in their legs from sitting too long.

Hawthorn also supplies the brain with more blood increasing the oxygen level. This helps improve your memory and your concentration.

Hawthorn seems to have a positive effect assisting to reduce high cholesterol as well as high blood pressure.

It is often used just as a relaxant as it is said to ease stress.

In many herbal products the leaves, flowers and berries are combined to take greater advantage of all the medicinal properties this plant has to offer.

The infusion of the flowers is particularly good for increasing the flow of blood to the heart, and when mixed with **yarrow**, can help relieve stress and hypertension. Juice from the berries can be expressed and used as a digestive aid, a cardiac tonic and to stop diarrhea. The decoction is made with 30 gr berries boiled in ½ litre of water for 15 mins, then allowed to steep for 10-15 mins. Drink a cupful 2 or 3 times a day. For a tisane wash the berries or flowers and leaves thoroughly and the pour a cupful of boiling water over them and allow them to steep for 15 mins before straining and drinking.

CHOCOLATE LIQUEUR FROM HAWTHORN BERRIES

Ingredients
1 bottle brandy
1 kilo hawthorn berries, washed and cleaned
3 large bars of chocolate

Method
Steep the berries in the brandy for a month, turning the bottle upside down once a day for two weeks. Leave in a cool dark place for the whole month.
Strain the berries and reserve.
In a heavy pan, melt the chocolate, then remove from the heat and stir the mushy berries into it so that they are well mixed.
With a metal spoon, scoop out the mixture and place on a greased baking tray. When you have finished, refrigerate so that the chocolate sets again. They are soon ready to eat. You also have hawthorn brandy, which is delicious too.

A word of caution to consider.

The white flowers that appear in the spring and the berries that cover the hawthorns in the fall attract insects, birds and other wildlife. Some of the wildlife may be desirable. But it can also be a disadvantage to have bees on the flowers if the hedges are near areas people congregate. Birds eating the berries make messes that can stain driveways or cars parked near the hedges. The berries themselves are a litter problem when they fall from the hedge onto the ground. The thorns make pruning the hedge a hazardous duty. It may also be dangerous to grow in households with children who play near the hedge. There are some thornless hawthorn cultivars available if you're doing it just to eat.

Maybe plant some Spanish bayonet to fill the gaps or diversify. Don't create anything that would give an intruder or burglar cover in your design though.

IMPROVING THE ODDS

This impressive clump of Spanish bayonet thrives in the hostile environs of a dry dusty bait shop parking lot in Woodville, Florida.

Spanish Bayonet or Yucca Aloifolio

Spanish bayonet may be the ultimate in "security plants" it can be planted beneath windows and other access points where its fiercely pointed leaves will prevent passage of all interlopers human and otherwise. Spanish bayonet has dark green, stiff, dagger-like leaves projecting from thick, trunk-like stems. This evergreen shrub can grow up to 15 feet in height, but often will flop over from its own weight

The leaves of Spanish bayonet are probably its most memorable feature, ending in sharp, needle-like tips. These spiked leaves have been known to pierce through even thick clothing, so select a planting location away from walkways and areas where people or pets could come into contact with the hedge. Plant Spanish bayonet as a security precaution, under windows and other areas of access, or as a living fence. Just be sure to plant it behind other plants, putting space between it and people.

The fragrant, bell-shaped flowers of Spanish bayonet are white with tinges of light purple, and appear in spring or summer on tall spikes at the center of the plant, high above the foliage. The blossoms are edible, making a crisp addition to salads raw, or served battered and deep-fried. Considered to be a luxury by the native North American Indians, the fruits were often baked in ovens. Spanish bayonet can be incorporated into almost any landscape in Florida (zones 8b-12). It has a high salt tolerance, making it an excellent choice for coastal gardens, and will grow in most soil types, as long as the soil is well-drained. It grows best in full sun to partial shade, but can tolerate nearly full shade.

Spanish bayonet requires little maintenance; it's highly drought tolerant and once established, requires almost no supplemental irrigation

Yucca flowers and fruits are edible fresh or dried. Traditionally, American Indians ate Banana yucca fruits raw, baked, boiled, or dried them, and ground them into meal. Once dried, they were often ground, and then kneaded into small cakes for storing. Among the Apaches, the banana-shaped fruits were gathered before fully ripe and laid on twigs covered with greens to ripen in the sun. When ripe, the fruit was roasted in hot ashes. The skin on the roasted fruit turned black and was easily pealed away.

The baked pulp was then spread on leaves to dry for two days in the sun, and covered with fresh sunflower blossoms. Pulp - Roast whole fruits until tender, scrape out pulp and remove seeds. Sweeten if desired. Use raw pulp for pies. Strain pulp and dry by boiling to a paste and finish in oven until a thick sheet. Eat dry or dissolve for a beverage. Leaves and flower stalks: The tender central leaves were also cooked in soups, boiled with meat, and used in a variety of culinary combinations.

Harvest young flower stalks before buds expand and fruits as they are available late spring through summer. Cut young flower stalks into sections, boil 30 minutes or roast until core is tender. Peel off tough rind. Serve with butter, lemon juice and seasonings. Buds and flower uses(Same as, but not as tasty as soapweed's): Cover 1 cup buds or flowers with water and boil 15 to 20 minutes until tender. Drain and coarsely chop. Add with chopped green pepper to several eggs and a little milk. Cook like scrambled eggs. For salad, boil one cup flowers and buds as directed above. Drain, chop and cool. Add celery, chopped apple, raisins, nuts, cabbage and mayo as in Waldorf salad. Seeds: Roast seeds at 375 degrees until dry and crisp. Grind coarsely and boil as vegetable until tender.

Medicinal Uses: Early Americans used the saponin-rich roots and leaves as a shampoo to promote hair growth and to combat lice. These same saponins (precursors of cortisone) are responsible for many of the yuccas' traditional uses as medicine. Decoctions of the stems and leaves treated gastrointestinal ailments such as heartburn and served as a laxative. Also, seeds were roasted in ovens and used as laxatives. Poultices of the grated roots (sometimes applied hot) were used to treat sprains and cuts, and the roots, stems and leaves were used to prepare tinctures, salves and liniments to relieve the pain of arthritis and rheumatism.

Prickly Pear Prison

Once established, a cactus border will provide security, beautiful flowers (bees are drawn to them along with other insects), and fruit known as prickly pear and tuna. Each variety should be sampled for ease of handling and flavor. Some are simply too seedy. The leaf / pad has medicinal qualities (diabetes, lotion for burns…) and is fried and eaten (nopal, nopalitos). And there's no doubt that if one's family were in a survival mode, this fence is a dream come true – security and food.

Cactus and their fruits are a large part of Mexican cuisine. The wide, flat cactus pads ("nopales") are used in many Mexican main dishes such as salads, eggs and as a filling for other dishes. The cactus fruit, sometimes called a "Prickly Pears" are very sweet and can be eaten raw, right off of the plant. Depending on the level of ripeness, they can range from slightly sweet to syrupy sweet.

The standard prickly pear Opuntia makes a good fence if you use a spined variety. The spineless varieties cannot keep humans away unless they only know it from a distance.

The Cereus variety (columnar) grown about twice as slow but offer fruit as good as dragon fruit. Cereus is grown in the deserts of Israel as a commercial fruit in extreme environs.

Cactus fruit grows on the edges of the flat pads of the cactus, and are pear-shaped. They can range in color from green (less sweet) to red (very sweet) and orange shades in between. The little spots you see on them are not thorns, but they are covered in glochids which are like little hair-like splinters that can stick into your skin and are very painful and very hard to see. When picking a prickly pear cactus fruit, you must protect your hands. You can use thick gloves or an old towel folded into a couple of layers. Do not touch the fruit with your bare hands.

Preparing the Cactus Fruit

First, you will need to get the glochids off so that you can handle the fruit. (If you purchase the fruit from a store, these glochids should already be removed.) The glochids can easily be burned off over an open flame. Grip a fruit with a pair of tongs or stick it on the end of a fork. Slowly turn the fruit over the open flame. As the glochids burn off you may hear popping sounds or see little sparks fly off the fruit. Continue until the all of the spots are blackened, indicating the glochids are gone. Don't forget to get the top and bottom of the fruit, as the glochid spots are more concentrated there.

Cutting the skin of the Cactus Fruit

Begin by slicing about one-quarter inch off of the ends of the fruit. Then take your knife and slice the skin of the fruit lengthwise across the top, about one-quarter inch down into the fruit.

Removing the skin from the Cactus Fruit

Use your fingers to pull the skin back off of the fruit. The skin is thin on the outside, but has a thick layer underneath that comes off too. Peel all of the skin off so that you are left with just the interior pear-shaped piece of fruit.

Serving the Prickly Pear

Now that the skin is removed, you can slice up the prickly pear to eat. The prickly pear has small, hard seeds that you cannot bite through, but they are safe to swallow if you prefer. Or you can chew on the fruit and seeds and spit the seeds out. You can also use a juicer or strainer to remove the seeds.

Apart from the unusual name, appearance, and origins of this fruit, it also has a very unique composition of nutrients, including high levels of vitamin C, B-family vitamins, magnesium, potassium, calcium, copper, and dietary fiber. In terms of organic compounds, prickly pears have high levels of flavonoids, polyphenols, and betalains, all of which have a positive impact on human health.

Health Benefits of Prickly Pear
It Boosts Immunity!

A single serving of prickly pears contains more than 1/3 of your entire daily requirement of vitamin C. Also known as ascorbic acid, vitamin C plays a major role in the immune system, stimulating the production of white blood cells and acting as an antioxidant throughout the body. Furthermore, vitamin C is an important component of various enzymatic and metabolic processes, including the creation of bone and muscle tissue

Strengthens Bones and Teeth

Calcium is an integral part of the human diet, and prickly pears contain a significant level of calcium in every serving.

Check your homes security features like dead bolt locks on all outside doors etc. and consider some of the multi locks that are used in Europe at this time. Most countries have such strict defense and gun laws that a strong door and the strongest lock possible are their only safety.

These locks are basically at least three multi position deadbolts operating off of one latch. If your budget can't afford this, a regular cheap strong barrel bolt strategically placed works wonders. Take a look at your door before adding one and consider if you want to run it from the door down to the floor.

Every house and door is different but this can really add to the strength and impenetrability. One thing most people never think to do is add a bolt or lock to hall doors. If you have to retreat or want to section off the house to slow someone down this becomes a key element in your defense. In a survival situation where break ins and home invasions are occurring regularly consider putting broken glass on the outside of your windowsills. You can powder the glass also, it will be invisible almost and anyone peeking in that lays a hand on it will leave bloody finger prints alerting you to a prowler. Please note it's illegal to do this trying to catch a stalker, peeping tom etc. in normal times. Like everything in this book the disclaimer do at your own risk applies.

Whatever you do always be sure to allow yourself an escape route though. Broken bottles embedded in concrete on the top of a wall offer visual and physical deterrence as well. Keep in mind these days this might be illegal to do in your area though.

3

Food Procurement

I guess you would say that this chapter is the reason you bought this book and you are wondering what the big secret is to surviving in a backyard. There is no secret to it; it's just the way you apply survival knowledge to your environment. I guess if you want to call it stage one of your preparedness plans you could.

My prepper survival knowledge dictates to me something rather obvious, well to some degree anyway. Consider that like me you have rarely ever seen a backyard that didn't get some kind of an occasional bird visiting. That's the secret of living in your backyard if you want to call it that. It might sound unappetizing, it might sound mean but bird is what is for dinner. Most likely small birds barely worth messing with sometimes but its protein and it changes a little bit with the season.

Itty bitty birds and wild weeds don't make much of a meal but you can get by on them. Keep buying rice and beans and storing them properly. Bird disguised as chili, tacos or some kind of Chinese food creations with soy sauce etc. added is the way to look at this self delivering survival food positively.

Remember that I told you this before you go all squeamish or undedicated trappers on me.

"The ability for a prepper to catch birds is an absolute necessity, because if you can't catch a bird you're going to be reduced to eating what they eat, which includes worms and bugs to survive."
Ron Foster

Now then, we got that out of the way and you know now beyond a shadow of a doubt that last Ron-ism told you a basic truth. That is why we theorize that, at least for a little while we can survive in a backyard sized area with some degree of guarantee for food.

The most important thing for you to do to prepare for using traps or snares to supply food is to educate oneself on the habits and lifestyles of the animals in your area. Observe birds in your backyard, in the wild and in different seasons. Learn their habits and habitats.

Trapping birds is illegal in many states so be aware not to do this except in a survival situation.
Trapping birds for survival is a viable source of essential calories in the wilderness as well as the backyard in a truly grid down no alternative situation.

Basic Bird Catching

Now a pellet gun of some sort is a great thing if you have one already or can afford one. Do you need one? No you don't. Most backyards have plenty of birds around at various times of the day visiting and by watching them you will learn their patterns.

Most preppers don't have slingshots, the shooting skills or pellet guns and even if they did you have the safety and neighbor problems to contend with using one. You can't use rifles or shotguns for the same reason plus you are going to disintegrate them small things into nothing but feathers.

We see the following quotation in the US ARMY SURVIVAL MANUAL

"All species of birds are edible, although the flavor will vary considerably. You may skin fish-eating birds to improve their taste. As with any wild animal, you must understand birds' common habits to have a realistic chance of capturing them. You can take pigeons, as well as some other species, from their roost at night by hand. During the nesting season, some species will not leave the nest even when approached. Knowing where and when the birds nest makes catching them easier Birds tend to have regular flyways going from the roost to a feeding area, to water, and so forth. Careful observation should reveal where these flyways are and indicate good areas for catching birds in nets stretched across the flyways (Figure 8-4). Roosting sites and waterholes are some of the most promising areas for trapping or snaring.

Figure 8-4. Catching birds in a net.

Now what works easiest to catch a bird is a couple rat traps from your bug out bag. These squirrel sized ones sort of work for birds but a lot of times you will find the smaller mouse traps are better.

A lot of survivalists and preppers have a lightweight survival gill net in their gear. You can use these as a "mist net" for birds on their flyways but the mesh can't be too big. By observing birds you can see the flyways the birds tend to use to escape or come in to the birdbath etc.

Now rather than trying to remember every bird trap you have ever seen in a disaster try making and remembering these two in your backyard. Don't leave it armed!! Try it with just a pocketknife. Now it is much easier to drill a hole with a portable drill, a push drill, a big ass screw etc especially if your knife does not have an awl.

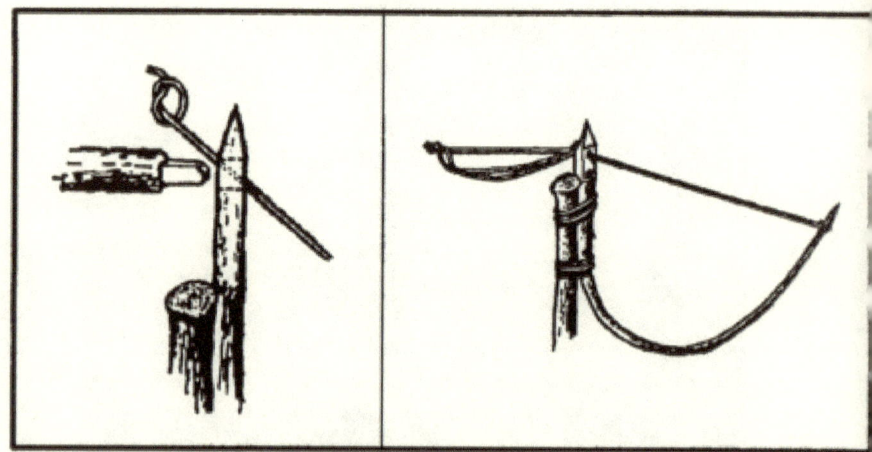

Figure 8-9. Ojibwa bird pole.

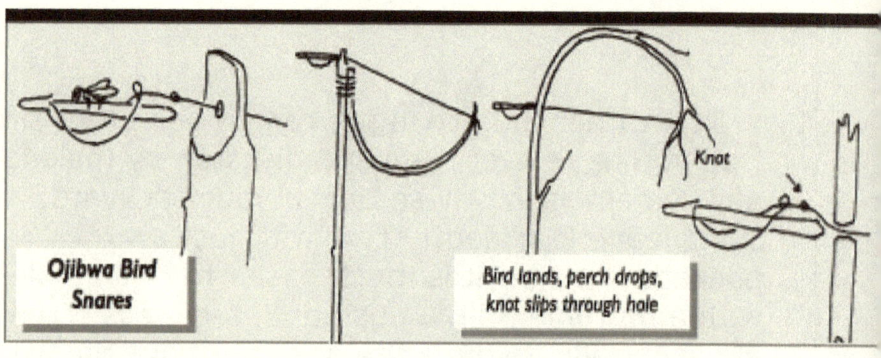

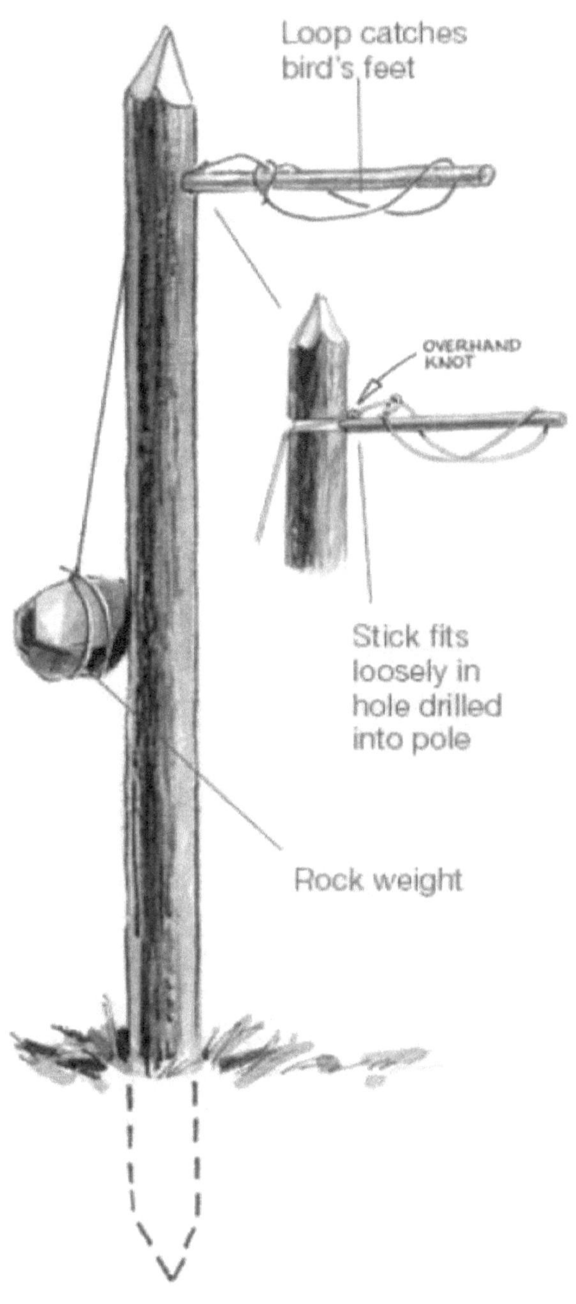

Loop catches bird's feet
OVERHAND KNOT
Stick fits loosely in hole drilled into pole
Rock weight

This works best when set in a clearing where the trigger stick offers a handy perch. The slightest weight on the trigger should cause it to fall and the noose to catch the bird by its feet.

1. Cut a 1/4-inch-diameter hole through one end of a stout 3-6 foot-long pole with a knife. If necessary, shave the sides of the pole to make it thin enough to make the hole. Sharpen the bottom end of the pole and drive it into the ground.
2. Whittle the end of the, about 6 inch, trigger stick so that it resembles a pencil with the point cut off. This end should fit loosely inside the hole in the pole.
3. Insert thin cord or fishing line through the hole and tie an overhand knot. Beyond the knot, form a slip noose. Tie the other end of the cord to a rock. Make the slip noose so that it drapes over the perch. Tension should hold it in position
4. Drape the noose over both sides of the trigger and insert it into the pole (if it's breezy, wet the cord with saliva to help it stay put). Draw the cord until the knot catches at the point where the trigger fits into the hole, to keep it from falling back through–until a bird alights on the small stick. When a bird flies down and perches, it will displace the stick, the rock will fall, and its feet will be caught as the loop quickly slides through the hole.

Now I told you this might cost you a few bucks, consider this while times are good and buy a couple of mouse traps. They can be had in a two pack for a dollar and some change. This could be a bountiful investment for when times get bad.

Grab one of these assorted packs of suet and seeds and nut bars for less than ten dollars at a Tractor Supply store. There is a years worth of bait and then some. Spend a couple of bucks and pick up a smallcage feeder that fits arund the bait block in case you want to use a whole one as a attractant or to just feed the birds and watch for now.

Quail noose

If you get lucky and have the bigger pigeons or doves etc. around this works. Works better if you funnel the bird into the snare though using brush etc.

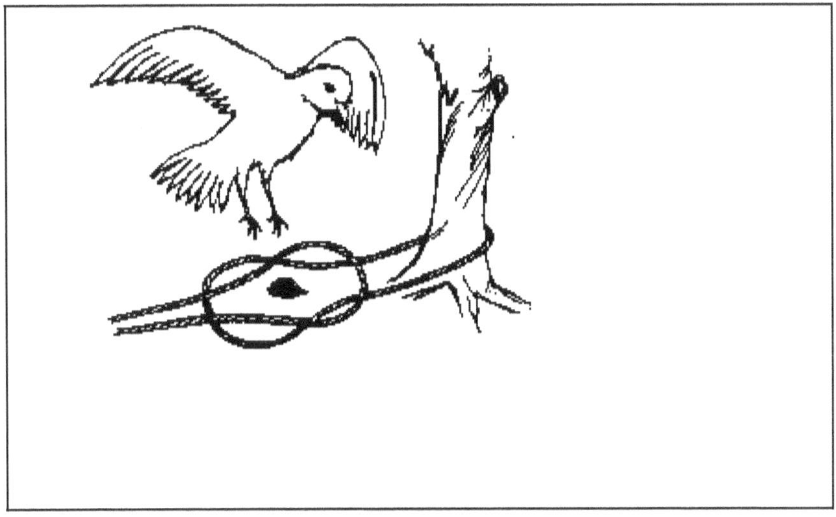

- The reef knot snare

This is one to try only if you have a lot of patience, a decent size bird and nothing better to do. You can, with a bit of ingenuity make it an automatic machine however. To do so would require an advanced knowledge or understanding of the principles and skills of trapping and snaring I detail in my other book called the Rural Ranger.

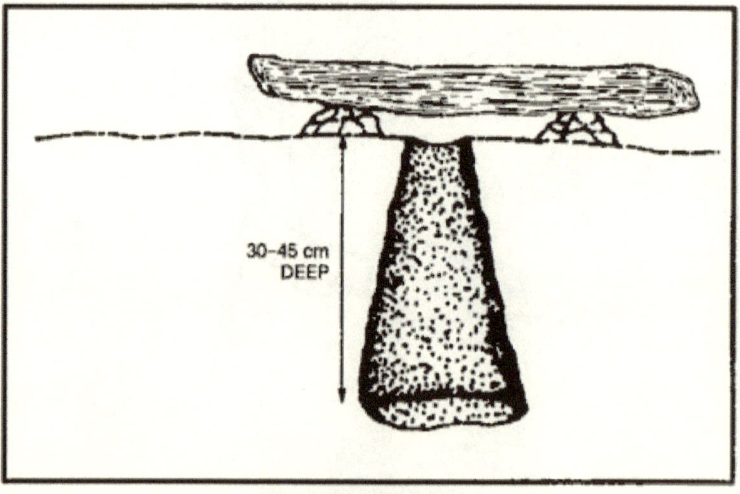

Figure 8-16. Bottle trap.

A bottle trap

A bottle trap is a simple trap for mice and voles (Figure 8-16). Dig a hole 30 to 45 centimeters deep that is wider at the bottom than at the top. Make the top of the hole as small as possible. Place a piece of bark or wood over the hole with small stones under it to hold it up 2.5 to 5 centimeters off the ground. Mice or voles will hide under the cover to escape danger and fall into the hole. They cannot climb out because of the wall's backward slope. Use caution when checking this trap; it is an excellent hiding place for snakes. You can also catch bugs for your bird traps.

Squirrels

One of the tastiest backyard delicacies but you will soon run out of tree rats to eat unless you start trapping the neighbor's house.

The squirrell pole strangle and dangle method works well and is easy to improvise.

What works the best is plain old peanut butter and a rat trap.

Make A Squirrel pole .Now 24 gauge or so brass wire works best for this or military trip wire but what if you don't have any wire?

No worries, you probability have more wire inside your house in the form of useless extension cords than you will ever need. Just strip the plastic off the wire and twist to make whatever size you want. A cheap pair of wire strippers comes in real handy for this chore/

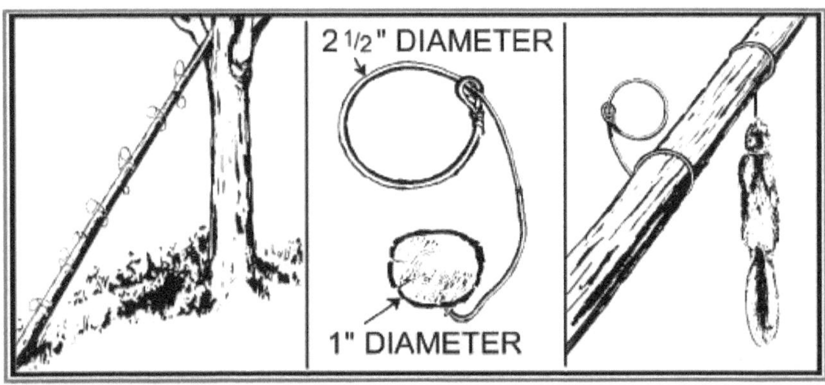

A squirrel pole is a long pole placed against a tree in an area showing a lot of squirrel activity (Figure 8-8). Place several wire nooses along the top and sides of the pole so that a squirrel trying to go up or down the pole will have to pass through one or more of them. Position the nooses (5 to 6 centimeters in diameter) about 2.5 centimeters off the pole. Place the top and bottom wire nooses 45 centimeters from the top and bottom of the pole to prevent the squirrel from getting its feet on a solid surface. If this happens, the squirrel will chew through the wire. Squirrels are naturally curious.

After an initial period of caution, they will try to go up or down the pole and will get caught in a noose. The struggling animal will soon fall from the pole and strangle. Other squirrels will soon follow and, in this way, you can catch several squirrels. You can emplace multiple poles to increase the catch.

Remove the entrails from smaller game by splitting the body open and pulling them out with the fingers. Do not forget the chest cavity.

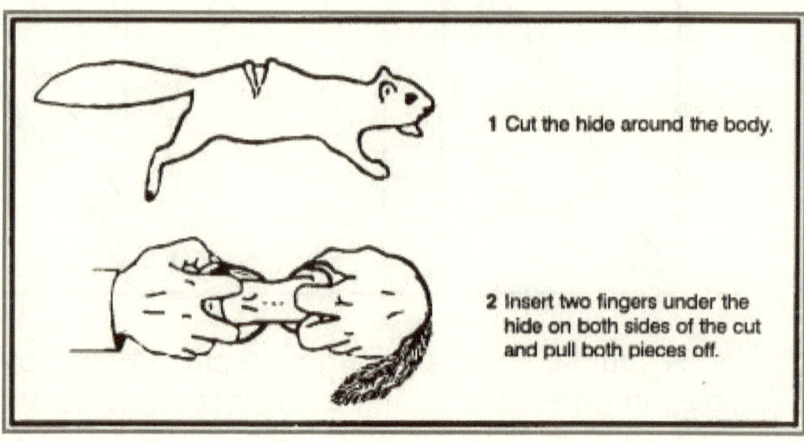

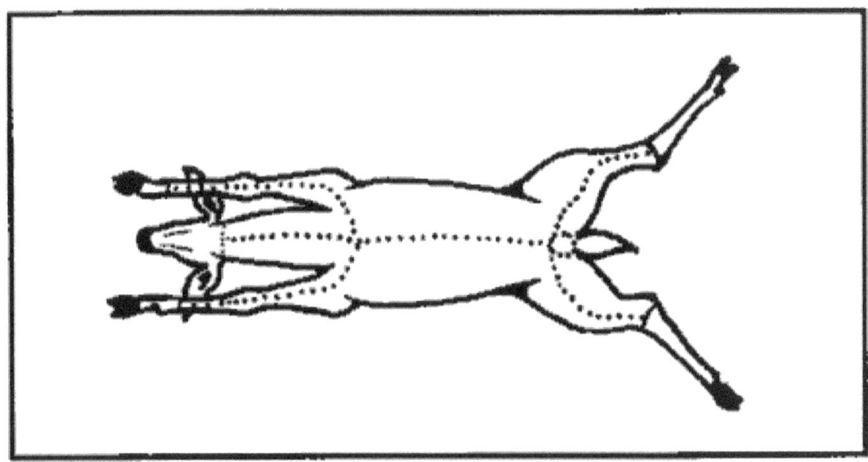

Figure 8-25. Skinning and butchering large game.

For larger game, cut the gullet away from the diaphragm. Roll the entrails out of the body. Cut around the anus, and then reach into the lower abdominal cavity, grasp the lower intestine, and pull to remove. Remove the urine bladder by pinching it off and cutting it below the fingers. If you spill urine on the meat, wash it to avoid tainting the meat. Save the heart and liver. Cut these open and inspect for signs of worms or other parasites. Also inspect the liver's color; it could indicate a diseased animal. The liver's surface should be smooth and wet and its color deep red or purple. If the liver appears diseased, discard it. However, a diseased liver does not indicate you cannot eat the muscle tissue.

Cut along each leg from above the foot to the previously made body cut. Remove the hide by pulling it away from the carcass, cutting the connective tissue where necessary. Cut off the head and feet.

Cut larger game into manageable pieces. First, slice the muscle tissue connecting the front legs to the body. There are no bones or joints connecting the front legs to the body on four-legged animals. Cut the hindquarters off where they join the body. You must cut around a large bone at the top of the leg and cut to the ball and socket hip joint. Cut the ligaments around the joint and bend it back to separate it. Remove the large muscles (the tenderloin) that lie on either side of the spine. Separate the ribs from the backbone. There is less work and less wear on your knife if you break the ribs first, then cut through the breaks.

Cook large meat pieces over a spit or boil them. You can stew or boil smaller pieces, particularly those that remain attached to bone after the initial butchering, as soup or broth. You can cook body organs such as the heart, liver, pancreas, spleen, and kidneys using the same methods as for muscle meat. You can also cook and eat the brain. Cut the tongue out, skin it, boil it until tender, and eat it.

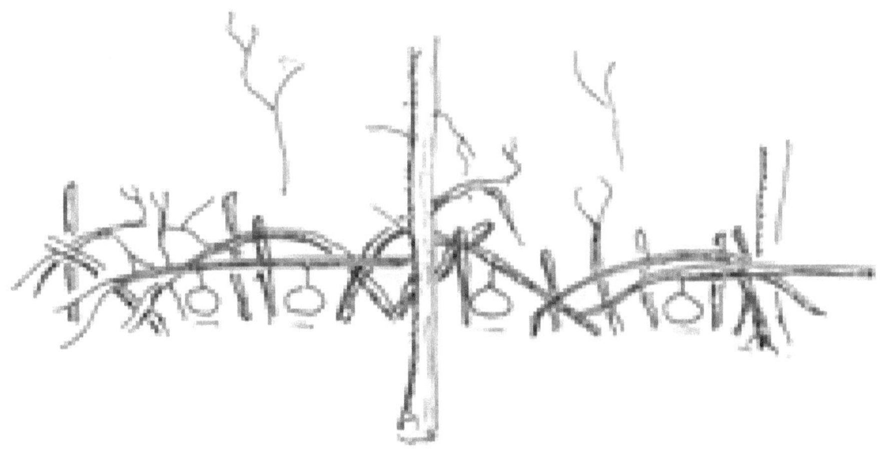

Now with a bit of resourcefulness and planning on your part a hedge row, fence line etc. can become a snare fence and critters can be either driven towards it or waited to try to wander through naturally. You would be amazed how many rabbits might be on a neighbor's lawn if you look early mornings or around dusk.

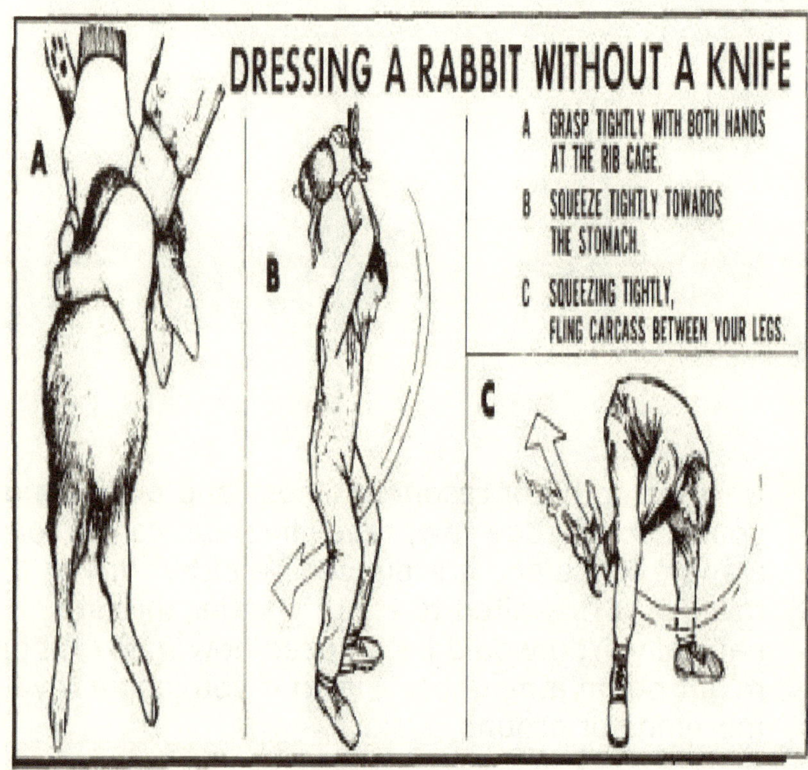

Figure 18-60. Dressing a Rabbit Without a Knife.

Smoking Meat

To smoke meat, prepare an enclosure around a fire (Figure 8-27). Two ponchos snapped together will work. The fire does not need to be big or hot. The intent is to produce smoke, not heat. Do not use resinous wood in the fire because its smoke will ruin the meat. Use hardwoods to produce good smoke. The wood should be somewhat green. If it is too dry, soak it. Cut the meat into thin slices, no more than 6 centimeters thick, and drape them over a framework. Make sure none of the meat touches another piece. Keep the poncho enclosure around the meat to hold the smoke and keep a close watch on the fire. Do not let the fire get too hot. Meat smoked overnight in this manner will last about 1 week. Two days of continuous smoking will preserve the meat for 2 to 4 weeks. Properly smoked meat will look like a dark, curled, brittle stick and you can eat it without further cooking. You can also use a pit to smoke meat (Figure 8-28).

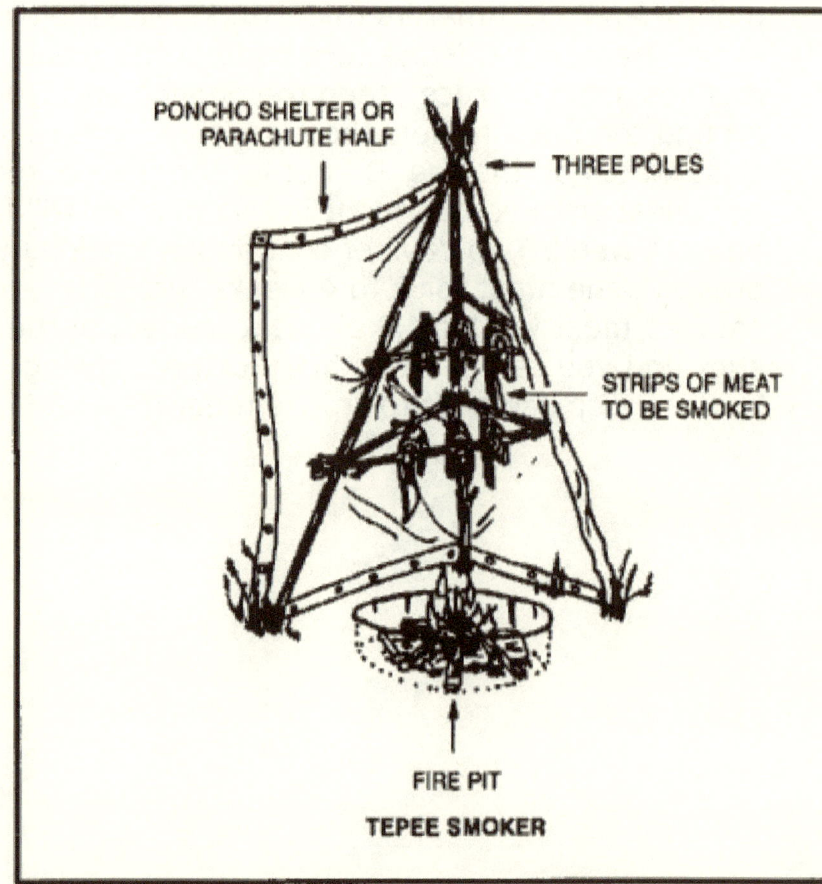

Figure 8-27. Smoking meat.

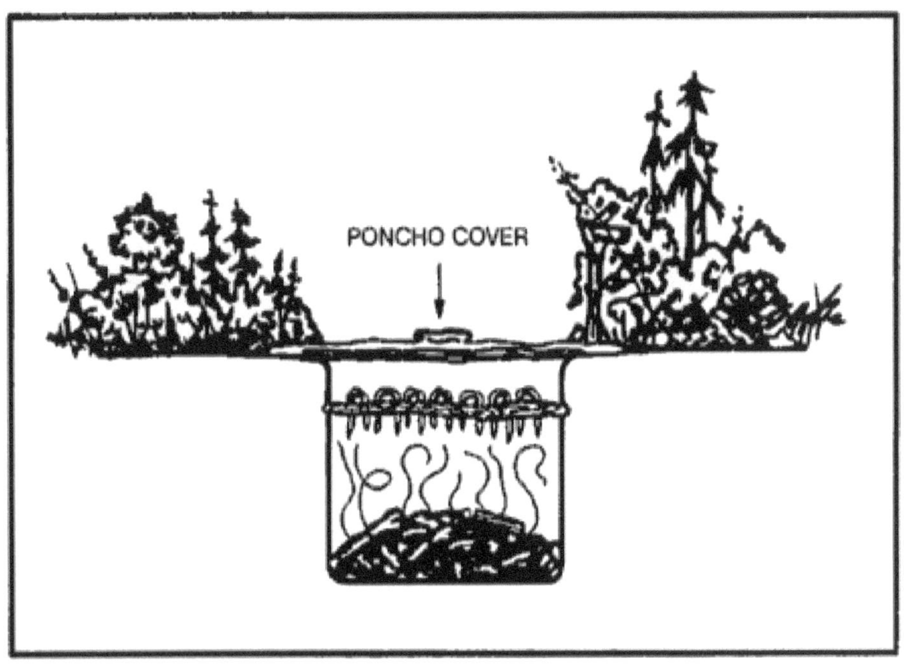

Figure 8-28. Smoking meat over a pit.

Drying Meat

To preserve meat by drying, cut it into 6-millimeter strips with the grain. Hang the meat strips on a rack in a sunny location with good air flow. Keep the strips out of the reach of animals and cover them to keep blowflies off. Allow the meat to dry thoroughly before eating. Properly dried meat will have a dry, crisp texture and will not feel cool to the touch.

Other Preservation Methods

You can also preserve meats using the freezing or brine and salt methods.

Freezing

In cold climates, you can freeze and keep meat indefinitely. Freezing is not a means of preparing meat. You must still cook it before eating.

Brine and Salt

You can preserve meat by soaking it thoroughly in a saltwater solution. The solution must cover the meat. You can also use salt by itself. Wash off the salt before cooking

WATER COLLECTION AND PURIFICATION

The **US Coast Guard** has done studies on the minimum levels of water and food in survival conditions. With a fresh water, a person can actually survive for anywhere between 8-18 days without food. There have been many documented cases where a human has lasted much longer than that in the right conditions.

HIDDEN WATER SOURCES IN YOUR HOME

Safe water sources in your home include the water in your hot water tank, pipes, and ice cubes. You should not use water from toilet flush tanks or bowls, radiators, waterbeds, or swimming pools/spas. You will need to protect the water sources already in your home from contamination if you hear reports of broken water or sewage lines, or if local officials advise you of a problem. To shut off incoming water, locate the main valve and turn it to the closed position. Be sure you and other family members know beforehand how to perform this important procedure. To use the water in your pipes, let air into the plumbing by turning on the faucet in your home at the highest level. A small amount of water will trickle out. Then obtain water from the lowest faucet in the home. To use the water in your hot-water tank, be sure the electricity or gas is off, and open the drain at the bottom of the tank. Start the water flowing by turning off the water intake valve at the tank and turning on a hot-water faucet. Refill the tank before turning the gas or electricity back on. If the gas is turned off, a professional will be needed to turn it back on.

EMERGENCY OUTDOOR WATER SOURCES

If you need to find water outside your home, you can use these sources. Be sure to treat the water according to the instructions on the next page before drinking it. ω Rainwater ω Streams, rivers, and other moving bodies of water ω Ponds and lakes ω Natural springs Avoid water with floating material, an odor, or dark color. Use saltwater only if you distill it first. You should not drink flood water.

WAYS TO TREAT WATER The instructions below are for treating water of uncertain quality in rare emergency situations in the absence of instructions from local authorities when no other reliable clean water source is available and you have used all of your stored water. If you store enough water in advance, you will not need to treat water using these or other methods. In addition to having a bad odor and taste, contaminated water can contain microorganisms (germs, bacteria, and viruses) that cause diseases such as dysentery, typhoid, and hepatitis. You should treat all water of uncertain quality before using it for drinking, food preparation, or hygiene. There are many ways to treat water, though none are perfect. Often the best solution is a combination of methods. Boiling or chlorination will kill most microorganisms but will not remove other contaminants such as heavy metals, salts, and most other chemicals. Before treating, let any suspended particles settle to the bottom, or strain them through layers of paper towel, clean cloth, or coffee filter.

Boiling

Boiling is the safest method of treating water. In a large pot or kettle, bring water to a rolling boil for 1 full minute, keeping in mind that some water will evaporate. Let the water cool before drinking. Boiled water will taste better if you put oxygen back into it by pouring the water back and forth between two clean containers. This will also improve the taste of stored water. You can use household liquid bleach to kill microorganisms. Use only regular household liquid bleach that contains 5.25 to 6.0 percent sodium hypochlorite.

Do not use scented bleaches, color safe bleaches, or bleaches with added cleaners. Because the potency of bleach diminishes with time, use bleach from a newly opened or unopened bottle.

Chlorination 11 Add 16 drops (1/8 teaspoon) of bleach per gallon of water, stir and let stand for 30 minutes. The water should have a slight bleach odor. If it doesn't, then repeat the dosage and let stand another 15 minutes. If it still does not smell of bleach, discard it and find another source of water. Other chemicals, such as iodine or water treatment products (sold in camping or surplus stores) that do not contain 5.25 to 6.0 percent sodium hypochlorite as the only active ingredient, are not recommended and should not be used.

METHODS OF WATER PROCUREMENT

Your first efforts in a survival situation should be directed towards establishing a good water supply. Initially you should look for ground water using the following methods.

Creek beds

Are easily discernible in dry areas because of the relatively green vegetation and taller trees following the course of the creek. Unless there has been recent rain in the area the creek bed will probably be quite dry.

You may be lucky enough to locate damp sand or mud at the bends of the creek or by digging in the creek bed at a likely spot. Water can be extracted from the damp sand or mud by soaking a rag in soil and wringing out the water into a container.

The exposed tree roots in the creek bed can be cut in lengths and drained of their fluid early in the morning. To reduce the risk of infection, any surface water must be boiled.

Rock Formations

If there is any water seepage from the ground, it is usually to be found near rock

formations, where the country is rugged and undulating. It may also be found in

some apparently dry areas. Rocky areas are ideal for rain catchments. Rain soaks

very quickly into the soil, whereas it can lie in pools on a rocky surface for some

time.

Salt Lakes

After rain has fallen, the top 3 mm of a salt lake is fresh water.

Animal Trails

Animals need water the same as humans and they will travel great distances regularly each day, leaving trails to the water source. Where a large number of trails converge together, it would indicate that the water was not far distant.

Water seepage

Natural springs and soft rock erosion areas [slopes, banks, etc.]

Coastal Water Sources

You can obtain drinking water by digging high up on the beach above the tidemark or behind the first sand hills. It tastes brackish and should only be used in small quantities.

Dew

The collection is tedious, but of some value in heavy grassland. Tie clumps of grass, a sponge or cloth around ankles and walk around in dew-drenched grass at dusk or dawn.

Squeeze moisture into a container and repeat. If you have a vehicle, wipe down the vehicle with a cloth.

Transpiration Method

Water can be obtained by placing **clear** plastic bags over the leafy branch of a nonpoisonous tree and securing the end of the branch. Ensure there are no holes in the bag [seal these with duct tape, band-aids, etc.]. The action of the sun on the plastic will cause water to be drawn from the leaves and run to the lowest part of the bag. Do not disturb the bag to collect the water, simply cut a small hole in the bag then reseal it. The leaves will continue to produce water as the roots draw it from the ground.

The transpiration method

The water should be drained off every two hours and stored. Tests indicate that if this is not done the leaves stop producing water. Probably the heavy concentration of moisture-laden air reduces the effectiveness of the sun.

If there are no large trees in the area, you can break up clumps of grass or small bushes and place them inside the bag. The same effect will take place. If this is done the foliage will have to be replaced at regular intervals when water production is reduced.

Ensure these bags receive maximum sunshine at all times. Exposed roots can be tested for water content. Soft pulpy roots will yield the greatest amount of liquid for less effort.

Distilling Sea Water

If only salt water is available a distilling plant can be made. You will have to improvise and use containers that can be found or that you may have.

First you require a container of seawater and material to seal the container to prevent steam from escaping. Push one end of the tubing or rubber hose through this seal material and check to see that the seal remains intact while blowing into the loose end of the tubing. Place the container onto a fire and bring to the boil.

Steam will be forced through the tube where it condenses and fresh water will drip from the end, into another container.

You must remember that the steam is the fresh water and therefore you must trap the steam to get fresh water. Any improvised method will do even if you place an open container on the fire and bring it to the boil, and then arrange a small plastic "tent" on top of it. The steam will strike the tent, condense and run down to your container or containers.

NOTE:

Foil or similar materials can make a seal around the container by folding it into a cone shape with the tubing attached to the small end of the cone and placing the large end around the container, secure ends of cone with wire to make the seal. Run the tubing through a cooling agent [water].

Clarification

The water you drink should be as clear as possible. You must strain it to remove the suspended matter, etc. A good method of doing this is to make a filter from the leg of a pair of trousers. Into this place fine sand up to one third the length of the trouser leg, charcoal for the next one third and fill to the top with gravel, small stones, etc.

Hang the leg of the trousers in a tree or similar and pour in the muddy water. It will take a little time but clarified water will begin to seep through the filter and drip into a container placed underneath.

Sterilization

Because the water is clear does not mean that it has no bacteria in it. To make sure of this you must sterilize any natural water that you drink. To sterilize water you can use several methods; the easiest would be to put in sterilization tablets. The alternatives would be to boil the water or to use other chemicals that will neutralize any bacteria such as Clorox or Iodine.

Various Directions For Treating Drinking Water In Small Quantities

Clorox

In emergencies, or as a temporary measure, water from contaminated or suspected sources can be disinfected by chlorinating, boiling, distilling, chemical treatment or mechanical filtering. In an emergency, think of this (one-gallon of Regular Clorox Bleach) as 3,800 gallons of drinking water

Latest Ratio of Clorox Bleach to Water for Purification

4 drops regular liquid bleach per quart of water (older information says 2) stick too two unless it's cloudy or use your own judgment.

16 drops regular liquid bleach per gallon of water according to Clorox site

(Old FEMA reprints says eight) Most sources recommend adding 8 drops per gallon for clear water and 16 drops per gallon for cloudy water.

(8 drops = 1/8 teaspoon, 16 drops = 1/4 teaspoon)

1-teaspoon regular liquid bleach per 5 gallons of water

Mix well; wait 30 minutes. Water should have a slight bleach odor. If not, repeat and wait 15 more minutes If the chlorine taste is too strong in the water after disinfecting, pour it from one clean container to another several times. This will drive some of the chlorine off as a gas, lowering the level of chlorine in the water and improve its taste.

(Only use Regular Clorox Bleach (not Fresh Scent or Lemon Fresh).

Since liquid chlorine bleach loses strength over time, fresh bleach should be used as a water disinfectant. If the bleach is a year old the amount should be doubled. Two-year-old bleach should not be used as a water disinfectant

Iodine dosage: using ordinary 2 percent tincture of iodine from the medicine chest, 3 drops per quart of CLEAR water, or 6 drops to each quart of cloudy water, and stir thoroughly, allow water to stand for at least 30 minutes before using or filtering for additional protection.

Aerobic Oxygen or Stabilized Oxygen One final chemical process, which might be considered, is called "Stabilized Oxygen". Adding Stabilized Oxygen to water kills hostile microbes, anaerobic bacteria and viruses. A wide variety of manufacturers are producing oxygen-enriched "concentrates" which, when added to water are intended to increase oxygen levels in the body but also act as a mechanism for killing bacteria. Some of the products on the market include Aerox, Genesis 1000, Dynamo 2, Aerobic 07, Aquagen and others.

This stuff can also be used for Tooth Decay & Gum Infection...2 to 3 drops on toothbrush Mouthwash... 10 drops per 1/2 ounce of water and gargle for 60 seconds, the manufacturers usually have a brochure with several uses packed with the product when you purchase.

There are a lot of reports to indicate that these products are quite effective in treating water, without the possible side effects of iodine or chlorine/Clorox.

Remember boiling is best and if you are stocking up on water purification pills etc. than go with variety so that your system doesn't get over exposed to any one chemical if you use long term and heavily.

(a) Secure safe drinking water from an approved or emergency sources if possible. If not possible, treat all water before drinking.

(b) If tap water is not clear, it should not be used. If a less turbid water source cannot be located, allow the water to stand in a container until the sediment settles and pour off (decant) the clear water into a clean vessel. Be sure to drink what you need today and try to find more tomorrow.

Home Made Water Field Filter

Find a suitable container such as a coffee can or bucket. Really any size cylinder can or will work your just limited in the amount of a batch you can run through and filter. Make a hole into the bottom of the can. This hole shouldn't be too large, because you don't want the water to run too fast through your filter. The More time the more filtered. Cover the hole in the bottom with a layer of fabric and then pour a layer of clean sand over that.

The most important layer follows next is grained charcoal from your campfire.

This layer should be the thickest. It is responsible for killing the germs. Sand and fabric are for the mechanical cleaning of the water. Above the charcoal add sand and fabric again. Now you can use your filter by pouring some water in through the top and after several minutes the filtered water will trickle out. Start by pouring an amount of water that equals too about two-thirds the size of the can you are using. You can make your homemade filter more functional and last longer by pre-filtering the water through a coffee filter before pouring

Distillation

While boiling or chemical treatment will kill most microorganisms in water, distillation will remove microorganisms that resist these methods, as well as heavy metals, salts, and most other chemicals. Distillation involves boiling water and then collecting the vapor that condenses back to water. The condensed vapor will not include salt or most other impurities. To distill, fill a pot halfway with water. Tie a cup to the handle on the pot's lid so that the cup will hang right side-up when the lid is upside-down (make sure the cup is not dangling into the water), and boil the water for 20 minutes. The water that drips from the lid into the cup is distilled. (See illustration.) Distillation

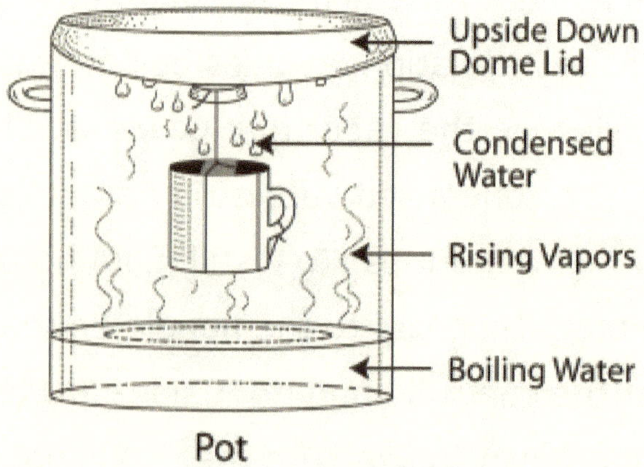

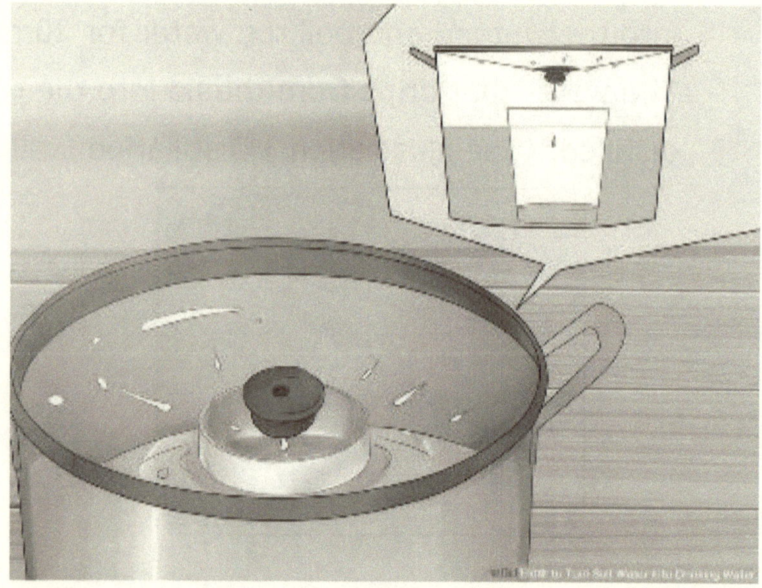

To distill, fill a pot halfway with water. Tie a
cup to the handle on the pot's lid so that the cup
will hang right side up when the lid is upside-down

(make sure the cup is not dangling into the water) and boil the water for 20 minutes. The water that drips from the lid into the cup is distilled. You can also use a rag on top of a steaming pot and then ring out the water it collects or cut down a liter bottle and have the rising steam hit the sides of it and trickle out the neck of the bottle. You can also run a copper tube from your kettle to another pot. It doesn't have to look like a moonshine still with many curves just one or two is enough or even a large arc from one container too the next will work. Could be your sinks faucets are hooked up with copper pipe; usually there is a hot and cold line. Have a look and a pair of channel lock pliers or monkey wrench etc. available if you have the need to scavenge...

☐Boiling -The water may also be purified by boiling. In this method, bring the water to a full boil for at least five (5) minutes. Cool and aerate the boiled water by pouring it through the air from one clean container to another, or by mixing rapidly with a clean utensil. Aeration will reduce the flat taste that is caused by boiling.

☐Using water purification tablets. (Follow the directions provided on package.)

One of the above treatments should be continued until water of unquestioned quality can be secured. Remember that color, odor, or taste cannot judge the safety of water. The organisms that cause water-borne disease cannot be seen.

Solar Stills

Below Ground Still

Solar Stills operate on the same principles that produce rainfall. The sun is allowed into and trapped in the Still. The high temperatures produced destroy all pathogens. The water evaporates, and in this process, only pure water vapor rises in the Still, only to condense on the plastic.

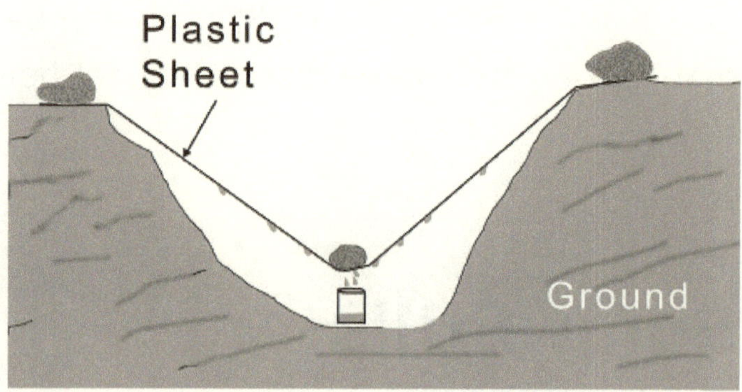

The solar still can provide water in survival situations. A clear piece of plastic allows the sun to evaporate ground water, traps it, and lets it trickle down into a waiting container.

To build a solar still you will need a piece of clear plastic sheeting at least 3 foot
(5 Ft is optimal) across. You will also need a container or something to hold water. A hose long enough to reach from the container to above ground is very good to have so add one to your survival bag.

You start by finding a low area where water is most likely to be underground failing this at the base of a slope works. This method works in deserts so you can't go wrong picking an area but the idea is to get optimal water out so pick the best likely area. The area should also get a lot of direct sunlight most of the day. Dig a bowl shaped hole big enough so that your plastic sheet will overlap the edges a few inches on all sides. About three feet wide and two-foot deep is considered optimal, so carry at least 5ft square size sheet with you if you can.

The cheap painters drop cloths available at hardware stores work well too and are already pre-folded for you. Dig the hole with sloping sides about the equivalent of 2/3 deep, as it is wide. Make the sides of the hole a little higher than the surrounding ground. In the bottom, dig out a hole of the correct size To place the bottom of whatever size container you have to hold it upright. Next, place your container, pot, can or other collection device for holding water in the center of the hole you dug at the bottom. If you have a hose, or some tubing, secure one end to the edge of the container so that it touches the bottom of the collection vessel and run the other end over the top of the hole.

Tie a loose knot in the tubing to help anchor it in the pot. Be careful to keep both ends free from dirt. This hose will allow you not to disturb your still as much and is for drinking out of as a straw.

Place the plastic sheet over the hole and put rocks and/or dirt on the edge to hold it secure. Find a smooth rock and place it in the middle of the plastic so that it is centered over your container and is about 15 inches below ground level. Gently push the plastic down until it has a good cone shaped slope (about 30°) to form an apex over the container if the rock is not already centered. Do not allow the plastic to touch the dirt except at the very top edge of your hole; don't let it touch the sides of the hole because the earth will absorb the condensed water.

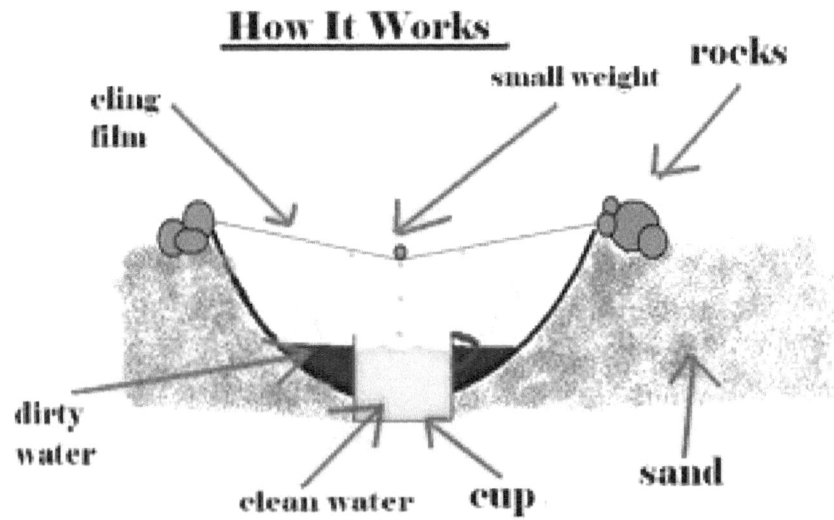

If everything is set up correctly, your still should begin collecting water within a couple of hours. You will notice condensation from evaporated ground water forming on the inside of the plastic sheet. When enough water collects on the sheet, it will trickle down to the center and drip into your container. If you have a hose in place, you can suck the water up without having to remove the plastic.

To enhance water collection, you can place cut foliage on the sides of the hole with the cut side facing towards center. Contaminated water, salt water, and even urine can be carefully placed on the side of the hole so it can evaporate and be purified. In case you use contaminated water, make sure it doesn't get into your container or touch the plastic sheet or hose.

If you do not have a container to collect water in like a pot or cup, try forming one out of a waterproof material like plastic or aluminum foil. If you have the resources, you can set multiple stills up in different areas to collect more water.

If polluted water is your only moisture source, dig a small trough outside the hole about 10 inches from the still's lip. Dig the trough about 10 inches deep and 3 inches wide. Pour the polluted water in the trough. Be sure you do not spill any polluted water around the rim of the hole where the plastic sheet touches the soil. The trough holds the polluted water and the soil filters it as the still draws it. The water then condenses on the plastic and drains into the container. This process works extremely well when your only water source is salt water.

You will need about three 3ft stills to meet all your individual daily water intake needs if this is your only source. Depending on your area and weather you use vegetation etc. will determine what your return per still is.

This also works if you have access to kitchen mixing bowls. Put Saran wrap over the top and a penny to weight down middle.

Pebbles work for weights also.

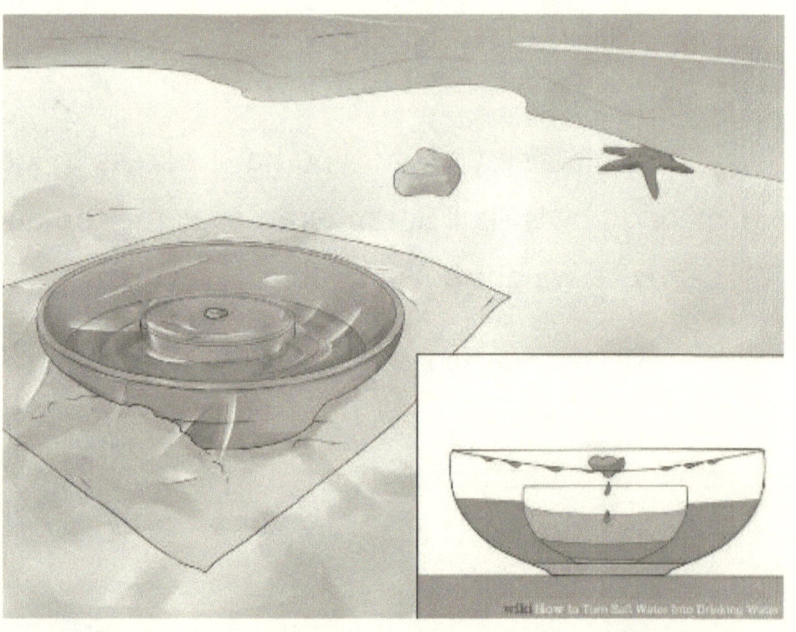

Grab you a couple salad bowls etc.

HEAT AND COOKING

There are many ways to cook when you do not have your oven, stove, or microwave:

1. Camp or fire pit (if it's not too cold to be outside)

2. Outdoor barbeque grill (gas or charcoal)

Don't get crazy now thinking cooking whole
hog!

3. Camp stove

4. Stoves that use denatured alcohol

Never cook indoors with gas grills, camping
stoves, or charcoal briquettes.

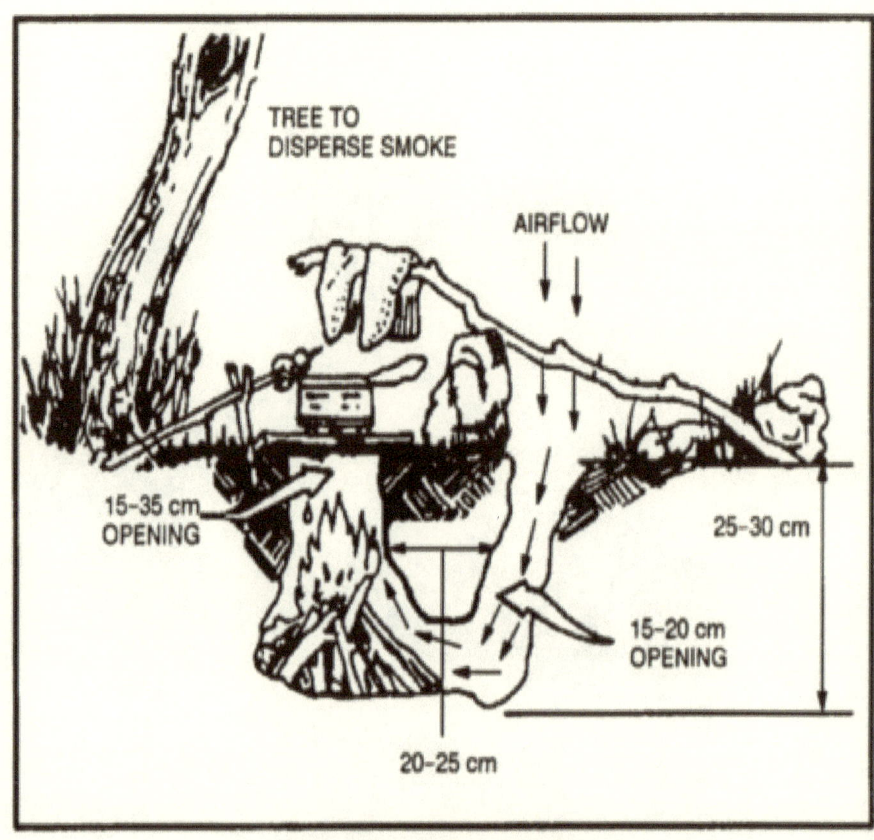

Figure 7-2. Dakota fire hole.

A **Dakota Pit Fire** is another way to make an efficient fire that uses very little fuel, and can warm you or food easily. Whereas it is contained in a hole, it is easy to hunch over it for warmth, or to place food or water over it for cooking. The second hole is to allow oxygen to get to the fire, thus preventing it from being easily smothered. It is scalable depending solely on the size of the pits you dig.

In some situations, you may find that an underground fireplace will best meet your needs. It conceals the fire and serves well for cooking food. To make an underground fireplace or Dakota fire hole (Figure 7-2) —

- Dig a hole in the ground.
- On the upwind side of this hole, poke or dig a large connecting hole for ventilation.
- Build your fire in the hole as illustrated

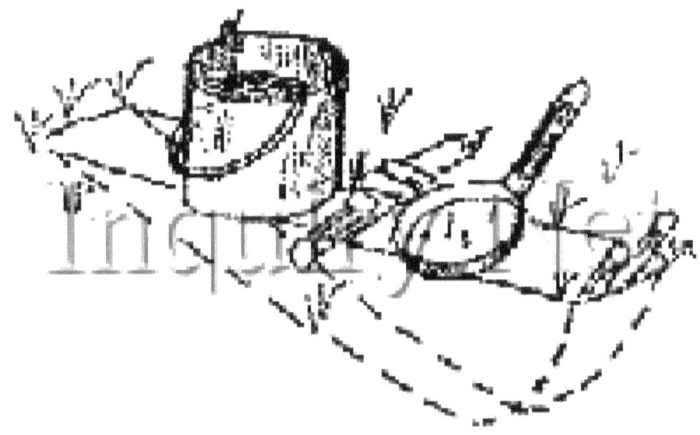

Trench Fire

This us the easiest way to adjust heat and cook multiple food courses.

Heat

A tin-can stove. A large can makes a good stove, cut stoke-hole and flue.

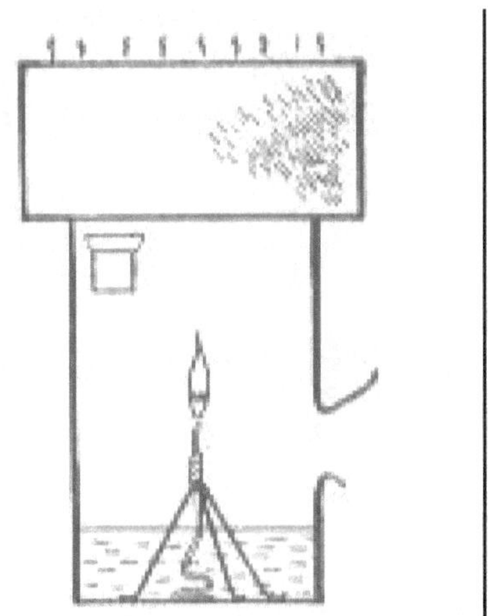

A tin-can heater that burns oil. wire tripod supports cord wick

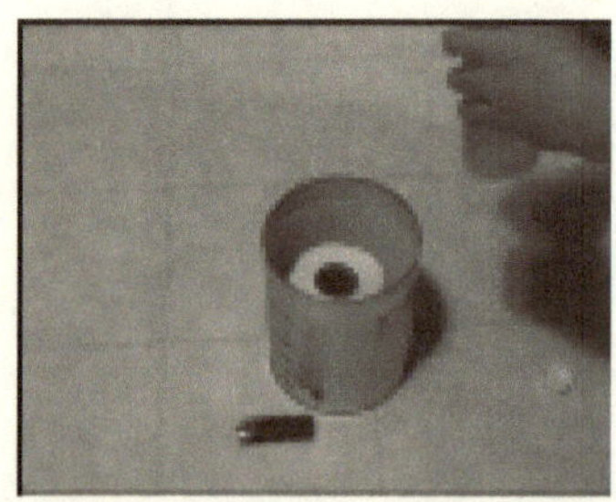

A toilet paper stove uses a roll and 90% rubbing alcohol as fuel for a car heater.

Now hands down the best backyard disaster cooker there is rocket stove. You don't have the time, resources or the energy to be gathering firewood everyday for a campfire. These things run on twigs or any other biomas. There is only one company to buy the best quality most technology advanced stove on the market from and that is Silverfire

 Introducing the SilverFire® Survivor 2nd Generation rocket stove with secondary combustion! This state of the art clean cook stove is durable, fun, and fast. Our Survivor uses minimal fuel, produces less char, low emissions, and minimal smoke using dry, quality biomass.

SilverFire® advanced designs maximizes improved efficiency and durability. Our focus is amazing & efficient cook stoves. Inefficient rocket stove designs sold by our competitors produce large embers and char. This is a sign of *inefficient combustion*, impeded ventilation, reduced heat transfer, and require more cleaning.

A well designed cook stove should produce only fine ash and burn clean! Compare our superior quality and advanced combustion technology compared to other brands of rocket stoves, and draw your own conclusions

This next one you can cook indoors with as well as create a heater if you put an iron griddle on top. This is the only portable woodstove on the market I know that could in emergencies heat a room in an apartment or house if you vented it out the window.

The **_SilverFire_® Hunter** is a lightweight, portable natural draft chimney stove designed for both indoor & outdoor use! The Hunter is a top lit updraft gasifier (TLUD), powered by twigs, yard scrub, or any flammable biomass (why buy fuel?).

TLUD's stoves utilize a batch fed combustion chamber. It is simple to operate. Just top light it like a candle, no continuous feeding required.

Vent the chimney outdoors to eliminate all household emissions. Insert vertical positioned fuel into the combustion chamber; next place a little tinder on top and light! To fine tune your flame adjust the ventilation door at the bottom of the stove. That's all there is to it! The portable *SilverFire*®Hunter model opens up a new frontier in biomass clean cook stoves. You now have the capacity to eliminate all household emissions! If you decide to buy one, tell them where you heard about them.

Sanitation

To build a makeshift toilet

If sewage lines are broken but the toilet bowl is usable, place a garbage bag inside the bowl. If the toilet is completely backed up, make your own. Line a medium sized bucket with a garbage bag and make a toilet seat out of two boards placed parallel to each other across the bucket.

An old toilet seat will also work. Use a 5 gallon bucket or its equivalent and knock a hole in it Towards the rim to fit a garden hose to it and seal around area with duct tape, this way when it is sealed the noxious odors can vent out a window etc. Line the bucket with lawn bags. There are many chemical toilet additives you can buy now as well as commercially made emergency or camping toilets you may want to consider adding to your disaster preparedness list. This seems to always be the last thing folks think of before a disaster and the first one after.

Decreasing the liquid from solid waste will decrease volume and making handling much easier. You can cover the waste with baking soda to aid in drying and to reduce odor.

If you and your family members can urinate in a separate container the bags will last longer. Dispose of urine down a drain and flush with water you have stored.

To sanitize waste

After each use, pour a disinfectant (see Disinfectants) such as bleach into the container. This will help avoid infection and stop the spread of disease. Cover the container or bag tightly when not in use.

To dispose of waste

Bury garbage and human waste to avoid the spread of disease by rats and insects. Dig a pit 2 to 3 feet deep and at least 50 feet downhill or away from any well, spring, or water supply.

If the garbage cannot be buried immediately, strain any liquids into the emergency toilet. Wrap the residue in several layers of newspapers and store it in a large can with a tight-fitting lid. Place the can outside until it can be buried.

Stock up now on insecticides as their numbers will increase greatly in this environment. If utilizing outside facilities a bit of quick lime added after each use is highly beneficial.

Thoroughly wash all dish and eating utensils with soap and hot water and sanitize after washing with a solution of one teaspoon 4-6% sodium hypochlorite (bleach) per gallon of water. If you must use cold water to wash dishes and utensils, rinse dishes with a solution of a tablespoon of 4-6% sodium hypochlorite per gallon of water. Better yet, use the disposable utensils you stocked up ahead of time. They will be safer if someone is ill or if there is no hot water.

Getting rid of the garbage

Sickroom waste should be handled very carefully and kept separate from regular garbage. Double bag sickroom waste and store it away from animal access until regular pick-ups are available. Compost bin outdoors for kitchen waste

Water substitutes for body cleansing

Rubbing alcohol

Lotions containing alcohol

Shaving lotion

Face creams and lotions

Towelettes

Wet washcloth to clean teeth, wash face, comb hair, and wash body

Makeshift shower - Use a spray bottle to shower; buy one of the camper's solar showers

Disinfectants** (Clorox Bleach Sanitizing Solution) Mix 1-tablespoon regular Clorox Bleach with one gallon of water. Always wash and rinse items first, then let each item soak in Clorox Bleach Sanitizing Solution for 2 minutes. Drain and air-dry. The best choice is a solution of 1 part liquid chlorine bleach to 10 parts water.

Other commercial disinfectants include HTH, or calcium hypochlorite, which is available at swimming pool supply stores; portable chemical toilets, which are available through recreational vehicle supply stores; and powdered, chlorinated lime, which is available at building, supply stores.

Commercial Water Pasteurization and Distillation
Products

□□Sunlight kills bacteria! Water in a capped 2-liter plastic bottle left lying on its side in strong sunlight for 4 hours will have very few live bacteria left in it.

6

FIREARM FOOLERY

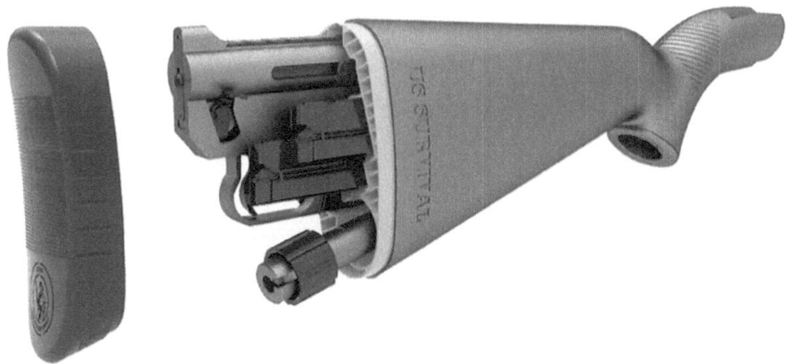

Now what prepper book is complete without a mention of guns? The Henry Survival Rifle pictured above is the perfect bug out gun as well as backyard survival tool. Not for shooting at birds or squirrels but animals of a size needing dispatch if you catch them in a snare. I will just leave you with the thought that pets are usually the first thing to disappear after a famine strikes. Enough said.

This weapon is accurate, reliable and affordable. It cab defend you well but for serious defense in just as small of package consider a folding shotgun. These single shots make great, kayaking, backpacking, truck guns etc.

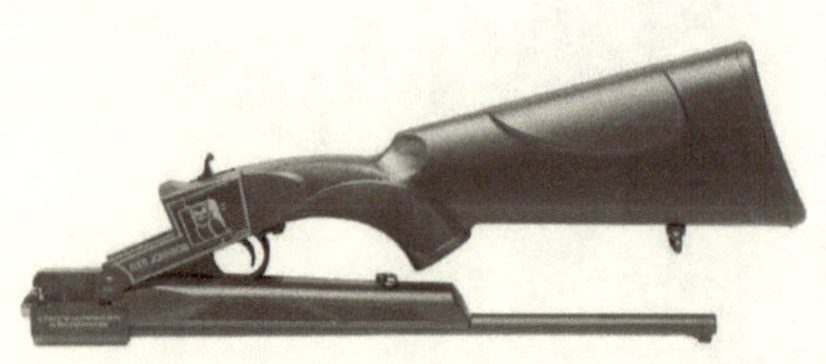

The Iver Johnson IJ700 Youth is bringing back the small bore shotgun tradition at a very affordable price. This Single Shot Break Action 20

Gauge Shotgun is becoming known as an ideal first shotgun for a youth or new shooter

Add a recoil pad and some ammo and all of it fits in its own laptop computer sized nylon tote bag.

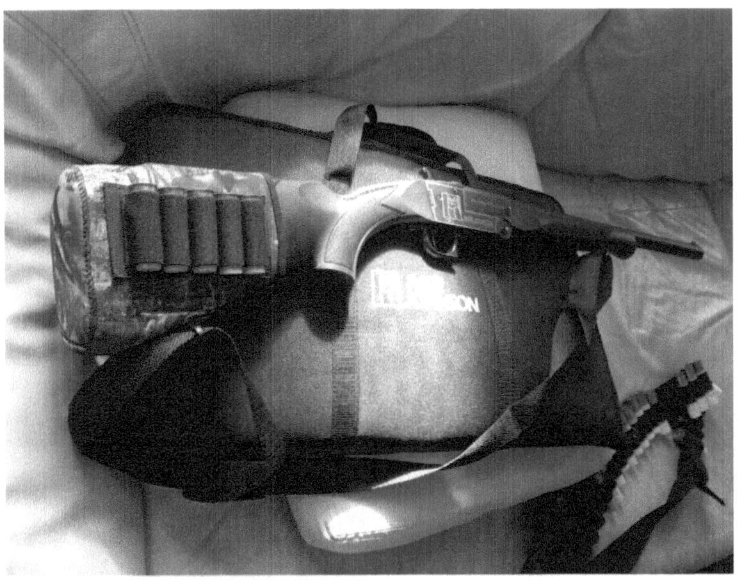

These two guns and my bug out bag are all I really need to bug in and stand a pretty good chance of making it all right. Yes I have an AR 15 but I don't feel under gunned with the two weapons/tools listed and they are more practical.

7

SURVIVAL SEEDS & SYMPATHY

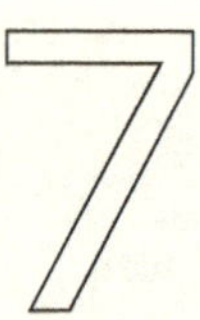

THE BUCKET BRIGADE

So get yourself a bucket suitable for a bug out but this one is for bug in gardening and put in it these items.

      (1)   box of Epsom Salt
      (2)   Box of Baking Soda

(3)   Bottle of Household Ammonia

(4)   Bottle of Castile soap or dish washing liquid

(5)   A couple quality empty spray bottles

(6)   This book inside a plastic bag

(7)   2 lbs of Contender beans

(8)   Entrenching tool

(9)   Ounce of butternut squash seeds

This do it yourself fertilizing kit will last you several seasons and if you are a practicing gardener be sure just to treat it as a backup prep and don't get into it unless truly necessary

Carry your other survival seeds if you got them in your pack where they will remain safe in case any of those liquids spring a leak.

That's it! Now then, you might want to add salt peter (Potassium Nitrate) from drug store, peroxide, hot sauce, and molasses, aspirin (Scientists have found that aspirin multiplies a plant's natural defenses against deadly viruses, bacteria, fungi and actually repels insects! For using this miracle drug in your flower beds and vegetable garden, mix 1 ½ uncoated, finely ground aspirin tablets and 2 TBS. baby shampoo in 2 gallons of water. Use a handheld sprayer and spray your plants every 3 weeks during the growing season.)

This do it yourself fertilizing kit will last you several seasons and if you are a practicing gardener be sure just to treat it as a backup prep and don't get into it unless truly necessary.

Now then you arrive on your impromptu relocation site and have picked you out a likely place to put in your bug out garden. (We will get into how to pick that out later.) You grab your handy dandy entrenching tool and fold it into an L shape and proceed to start digging like a dog with both hands on the shovel, feet splayed and bent at the waist.

HOME MADE MIRACLE GROW

DYI Miracle Grow

Ingredients:

- 1 gallon of water
- 1 tbsp Epsom salt
- 1 tsp baking soda
- 1/2 tsp of Household ammonia

Mix all ingredients together and use once a month on your plants or every couple weeks in poor soil conditions.

Shannon's Homemade Monster Tomato Fertilizer recipe:

- 2-3 dozen crush egg shells
- 2 cups bone meal
- 1/2 cup Epsom salts
- 14 crushed aspirin (a natural rooting hormone!)

Instructions for up graded homemade vegetable fertilizer

○ 1

Pour 1 gallon of hot water into a small bucket.

○ 2

Add 1 teaspoon of baking soda and 1 tablespoon of Epsom salts to the hot water. Stir until both ingredients have dissolved.

3

Pour 1/2 cup of molasses and 1/4 teaspoon of ammonia in the bucket. Stir again to combine all of the ingredients.

○ 4

Set the baking soda fertilizer aside until it cools to room temperature.

○ 5

Pour 1 cup of the homemade baking soda fertilizer into the soil of each plant. Repeat monthly to encourage your plants to grow healthy and strong.

Natural Alternative Fertilizers

I think it is safe to say most bug out locations as well as backyards will have access to have a bunch of leaves on the ground, they all work but here is a specific fertilizer recipe to help all you want-to-be bug out preppers out.

Oak leaves: Fill 1/3 of a five-gallon bucket with dry oak leaves and add water to the top of the bucket. Place the mixture in a sunny spot and let it steep in the sun preferably until the water takes on the color of iced tea (ideally for one week). If the entire wait seems to be too long then add boiling water to the leaves and use the solution once it is cold. Do not waste the left over oak leaves; use them to make a dandy mulch.

No trees? No problem in fact better fertilizer is made from weeds and other herbaceous plants.

WEEDS – You have literally got your own fertilizer growing under your own two feet**! Could be weeds are your ready made food garden also but we will get into that later.**

To just name a few of the many beneficial weeds you are likely to encounter are Nettles, comfrey, yellow dock, burdock, horsetail and chickweed make wonderful homemade fertilizer. There are several ways you can utilize green leafy matter to make your own brew or to help speed up your compost pile. Another thing to consider is if your weeds have not gone to flower you can cut them down and dry them in the sun to use as mulch. Weeds are high in nitrogen.

Borage (starflower) is an herb but for some people they say it's a weed. It has many of the same nutritional properties as comfrey. It is also said to increase the flavor of tomatoes and repel horned caterpillars. What you do is dry the entire plant, root and all, and put it in your compost tumbler or pile.

Borage helps break everything down and gives the pile an extra dose of heat. A jump start as it were.

Some folks let the weeds soak for many days in a bucket of water. For an extended brew, get out the bucket and your bandana! The bandana you might find you need for your nose because this technique gets rather stinky!

I am not in any way a fan of fermented fertilizers but if you want to take the "putrid plunge" and figure stinking stuff like fresh manure is worth playing with, place a bunch of weed leaves and roots in a 5 gallon bucket. Weigh down the leaves with a brick to ensure the plant matter is covered and add water to cover.

Stir weekly and wait 3-5 weeks for the contents to get thick and gooey. Then use that fetid smelling goo, diluted 1:10 or more as a soil drench fertilizer. To make it even more convenient, you can use two buckets and make a hole in the bottom of the bucket that contains the plants.

The sludgy goo will seep through to the lower bucket. Remember that it is always best to apply the liquid fertilizer diluted – it should look like weak tea.

You can use any combination of herbaceous plants to create fertilizer, put them in a container, fill with water, and cover with a fairly air-tight lid.

Leave it for a few days to a couple of weeks or months, and you have an herbal tea. Especially consider that if you forget about it for awhile that if you leave it for long enough that the bad smell mostly will go away, the resulting brew will contain many nutrients and beneficial microbes from the plants.

GRASS CLIPPINGS – this material is beneficially rich in nitrogen, grass breaks down over time and enhances the soil. **Fill a 5 gallon bucket full of grass clippings.** You can even add weeds! Weeds soak up nutrients from the soil just as much as grass. Add water to the top of the bucket and let sit for a day or two. Dilute your grass tea by mixing 1 cup of liquid grass into 10 cups of water. Apply to the base of plants using the same amounts as listed above in the urine recipe.

Keep in mind grass seed in the garden is not welcome and by the way if you ever try hay bale gardening and use wheat straw I can almost guarantee you will have a huge clump of wheat grass where it was sitting, so you may want that, I personally don't.

You don't have to spend hundreds of dollars buying fertilizer at the local gardening store. By using items around your house, you can make an effective vegetable fertilizer with little effort or money. Most ingredients used for homemade fertilizers are things you would normally throw into the trash or have on hand already.

Use your food scraps to grow healthy vegetables. Although plants will grow as long as they have soil, water and light, fertilizer can be used to help the plants grow faster and appear more vibrant. Store bought fertilizers contain chemicals that can burn the plants if not used properly.

It is much safer for the plants when you create a homemade fertilizer to use. This fertilizer should contain baking soda, which eliminates the growth of fungal diseases that will hinder the plant's growth. Backyard gardeners truly think that baking soda's anti-fungal properties are as good if not better than store bought chemicals.

ADDRESSING GARDEN PROBLEMS

Zucchini, tomatoes, potatoes, pumpkin, melons, cabbage, squash, flowers and even fruit trees can be killed or damaged by blight or powdery mildew.

How it works is powdery mildew is a fungus that will attack the immune system of a plant or it will enter a plant's most productive phase when fruit is just about ready to ripen.

If not treated in time, baking soda may not halt fungal attack plants but it will help to slow the advance of the disease and prevent its outbreak to other plants. Once you use baking soda in your garden, you'll always use baking soda.

Make a Spray to Prevent & Treat Powdery Mildew.

Powdery mildew can be a problem for many plants. Plants prone to damaging powdery mildew include cabbages, bergamot or bee balm plants, squash, zinnias, lilacs, mushrooms, tomato, etc.

Cucumber and Squashes are particularly susceptible to powdery mildew which can eventually affect the plants immune system and kill it off. Stressed plants also attract bugs out the wazoo.

There's nothing worse than watching your plant grow to maturity, bloom and fruit and powdery mildew kill it off. Just makes you sick to your stomach. A simple mixture of baking soda, water, and dish detergent can really save your cucumber crop or deter the mildew from even happening.

2. Sprinkle Baking Soda on Cabbages (and other Brassicas) to Thwart Caterpillars, Aphids, Ants, Silver Fish and Roaches and some beetles away. Put directly onto slugs to kill them. Caterpillars can wipe out an entire crop of cabbage within a few days. Aphids can multiply so fast that a cabbage can be unrecognizable.

Caterpillars are the worst garden offenders. Those cute and colorful worms are like punks in a mash pit. When your cabbage begins to look like Swiss cheese.. You know you have caterpillars and its time to break out the baking soda or other remedy.

Make a 50/50 combination of flour (don't matter if it is self rising etc.) and baking soda, and dust it all over whichever plants the cabbage worms are eating. The mixture is good for most vegetable plants particularly cabbage, broccoli, and kale plants which caterpillars love. They'll eat the combo while munching on the leaves and will die within a day or so. Repeat as necessary.

NOTE: The birds will enjoy the caterpillars for dinner!

Urine

The average adult produces about 1 1/2 quarts of urine per day. Diluted 1:20 with water, this would make about 7 gallons of high-nitrogen liquid fertilizer, so a family of four could produce enough high-nitrogen fertilizer to produce an average garden and lawn.

As the scientist Brinton suggests, when we think of N-P-K, we should also think N-Pee-OK! You might keep a designated bale of hay out in the garden for urine deposits. If you do this you can use the urine-enriched hay from "pee bales" as nutrient-rich mulches in your garden.

You can pee in a bottle or bucket, dilute it 20:1 with water, and then feed the plants or your lawn directly.

Ways you can use urine in the garden:

You can pee directly in the garden, too, I have often. Just make sure you don't pee right on your plants – ever notice how certain shrubs or patches of grass in dog parks turn yellow and die? It's not a great homemade lawn fertilizer, that's for sure – that is unless you dilute it first so think clear is cool and any other color needs second thoughts if direct from the source.

Urine should be used as fresh as possible to fertilize your plants, but if that's not always possible, put a lid on the jar or container immediately. Urine that's been left in the air for a while will be busy converting itself from urea into pure ammonia — your compost pile will still love it though.

For pouring around the roots of your vegetables and other plants, dilute 1 to 10 with water **(keep a handy watering can near the back door).** You should already be thinking about where you most often go at inopportune times, the call of nature will remind you that you don't like venturing far in early mornings and late nights. For younger plants and seedlings, dilute 1 to 20 with water, and for container plants dilute 1 to 30 with water.

Don't worry about getting the exact strengths exactly right, it's just that urine is high in nitrogen and has a lot of mineral salts in it, so it can burn plants. These salts are a good reason to try to avoid applying urine directly to plant leaves; it's best to pour it out in the soil around plants.

Apply weekly to fast growing and large plants, less often to very young and slower growing plants.

Your whizzer is the one thing you don't need to remember to pack! There are no doubts about the effectiveness of urine as a near perfect, soluble fertilizer on your garden.

I'll leave it up to you and your imagination how you go about adding urine around your plants or whether or not your aim is good. High in nitrogen, urea contains more phosphorous and potassium than many of the fertilizers we buy at the store!

Look that ratio of 1 to 20 is hard to think about when considering your bladder and a container if it ain`t marked and of sufficient volume to accommodate you unless it is give me a urine sample at the doc's and it seems you never have enough.

If you want to mix it mentally, a good ratio of urine to water would be 1:8. You can collect a cup of urine and pour it into 8 cups of water in a plastic bucket used outside for fertilizing plants.

Pour 2 cups around the perimeter of each SMALL plant. For MEDIUM plants add 4 cups and LARGE plants deserve a good 6 cups of your own personal home grown brew. Water with this soluble solution once a week or so water hydration supplies permitting.

Not too much or you will have all leaves and no fruit!

KEYHOLE GARDEN

A keyhole garden is a small organic vegetable patch which can efficiently provide plenty of food for your family. This design is typically used in Africa due to its water efficiency and reduces waste by incorporating a central composter to provide nutrients.

To forget how to dig the earth and to tend the soil is to forget ourselves. ~Mahatma Gandhi

Have you ever heard of a garden that waters and fertilizes itself? Keyhole garden A keyhole garden (so-called because of its shape) is a round raised garden, supported with stones

Is your backyard too hot and dry to cultivate the vegetables you have only dreamed of? Keyhole gardens were developed for the sole purpose of maximum crop output in the hottest and driest of conditions. Their low cost, low maintenance and versatility make them a desirable gardening option for your yard and for gardening across the globe.

A keyhole garden (so-called because of its shape) is a round raised garden, supported with stones. Keyhole gardens are built in places where it is difficult to build normal gardens (rocky areas, shallow arid/or compacted soils, etc), near the entrance of dwellings to facilitate their watering with household waste water. Keyhole gardens are made with low-cost locally available materials. The production of a keyhole garden can be enough to feed a family of 8 persons. Such gardens can produce food all year round even under harsh temperatures and can support the production of at least 5 varieties of vegetables at a time - thus supporting dietary diversity. Compared to regular vegetable gardens, keyhole gardens require less labor (ideal for elderly, children or sick persons), less water and no costly fertilizers or pesticides.

They act like an organic recycling tank, using your food and garden waste as fuel to grow vegetables! Crop rotation and growing of insect-repellent plants are important to balance nutrient demands, fight insects and plant diseases, and deter weeds.

Benefits of the Keyhole Garden

Soil enrichment
• The layers of organic materials decompose over time, adding nutrients to the soil.
• The central composting basket continuously replenishes the soil.

Moisture retention
• The layers soak up moisture, so the garden requires less water to remain moist.

Year-round vegetable production
• The stones of the keyhole garden wall absorb heat from the sun, protecting crops from cold winter temperatures.

Labor saving technology
• The soil re-nourishment and moisture retention reduce the amount of time required to maintain the garden.
• The garden shape makes it more accessible to sick or elderly gardeners.

Low-cost design
• All construction materials should be readily available (at no cost) to gardeners.
• Gardeners might need to purchase seeds for planting, however.

Steps in Construction of a Keyhole Garden

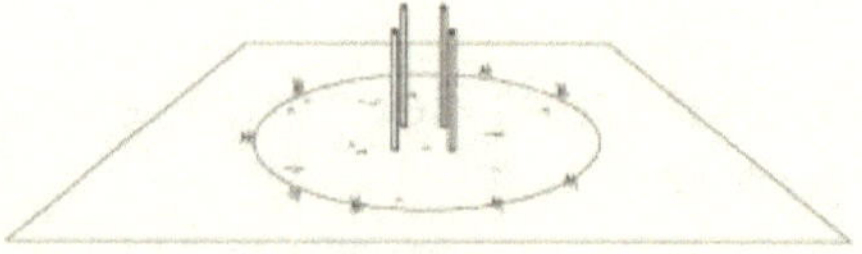

* A circle about 6 1/2 feet across is cleared.
* Four corner posts are secured into the ground.

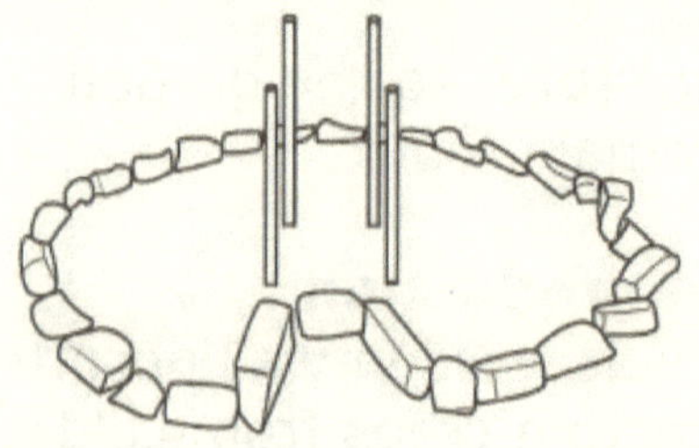

* The outline of the garden is marked with stones.
* The outline dips inwards at the center.

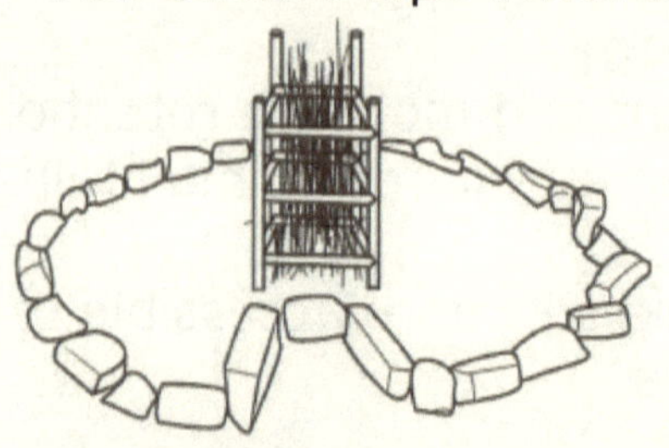

* The basket is encircled with rope and lined with thatching grass to allow water that is poured into the basket to flow into the garden soil.

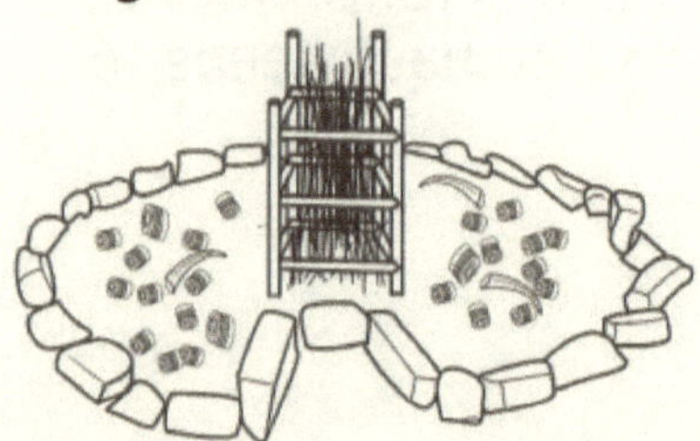

* The first layer of the garden is iron scraps such as empty food and

beverage cans, aloe leaves, dry animal bones, broken clay pots, which can be substituted with fist-size stones

• These materials provide minerals to the soil as well as drainage in heavy rains.

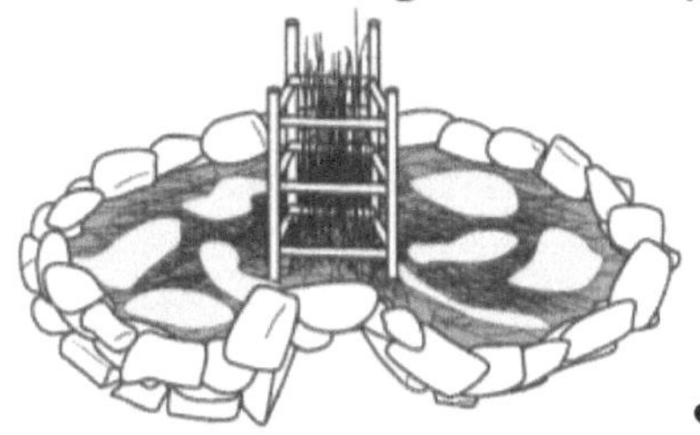

• The first layer is covered with soil that gives nutrients, thatching grass that retains moisture, and wood ash that provides potassium.

• Every layer should slope downwards from the basket so water can flow properly into the soil.

• Soil is added on top of the wood ash.

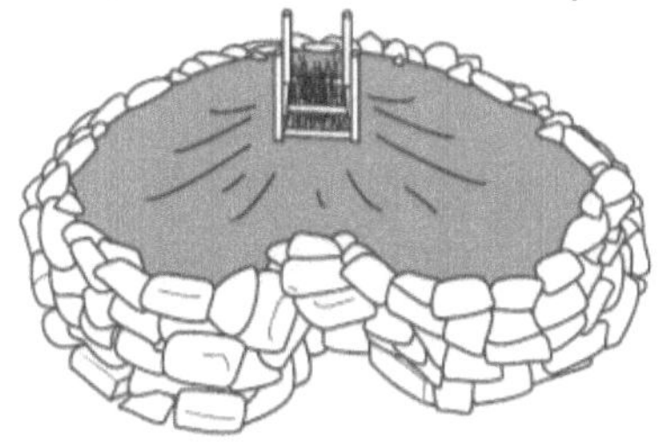

• Soil is added on top of the wood ash.

• A thick layer of mixed soil and dry manure is added on top. Using wet manure will kill young seedlings

• Add stones to the garden walls as the layers grow taller.

• Seeds are planted according to the season.
• During the winter, protect plants from the cold with thatching grass or old carpet. During the day, plants should be uncovered so they receive sunlight.

Planting Keyhole Garden

Space, soil nutrients, and pest management are key considerations in planning your garden. Companion planting is planting different kinds of crops together in the same garden in order to best satisfy those needs. Different methods include planting leafy crops next to root vegetables or planting pest-resistant vegetables (like onion or garlic) next to regular crops. To best ensure that your garden will
stay fertile and resist pests, plant a minimum of four vegetable types.

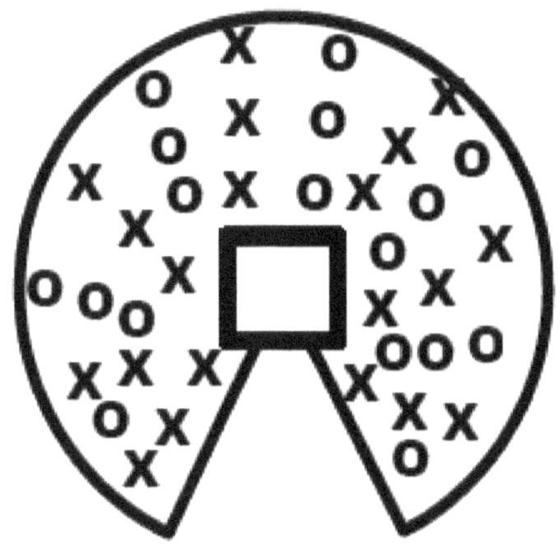

One idea for companion planting.
X: leafy plants
O: root plants

Preferred Crops For Keyhole Gardens

Root Crops

- Carrot
- Onion
- Beetroot
- Radish
- Turnips
- Garlic

Leafy Crops

- Spinach
- Swiss chard
- Lettuce
- Rape
- Mustard spinach
- Herbs

Crops *NOT* Recommended For Keyhole Gardens But I plant Them in Mine Anyway and have good luck, there are just easier ways to grow them and spreading plants take up a lot of space.

- Tomatoes
- Cabbage
- Peppers
- Eggplant
- Chilies
- Maize
- Peas
- Beans
- Potatoes
- Squash

Maintenance of the Keyhole Garden

Watering

- The garden should be watered regularly so that the garden soil is moist.
- Clean water is used on the topsoil.
- Water from washing hands, laundry, or dishes is poured into the basket. The thatch and the composting in the basket will clean the water.

Soil

- Dry manure and topsoil should be replenished in the garden so that it does not become sapped of its fertility.

Basket

- Uncooked vegetable scraps, dry manure, eggshells, and compost are added to the basket. These replenish the soil.
- The basket will decompose within 1 or 2 years and should be replaced.
- The garden wall near the basket can be pulled away, allowing gardeners to remove the old basket and replace it.

Garden construction

- Over time, the garden may lose its nutrients, and vegetables stop growing well. You then need to rebuild the garden. This is usually done every 4–5 years.

Why would I bother building one of these?

The ultimate answer, apart from the accessibility features mentioned earlier, is the efficient use of space. Consider creating a square, raised garden bed that you could access from every angle. It could only be 1m x 1m (3.3ft x 3.3ft) but would take up a space measuring 2m x 2m for access. Therefore, this one garden bed would require 4sq. meters but only provide 1sq. m of gardening plot. The arable portion of this plot is only 25%.

A keyhole garden, on the other hand – with the measurements quoted earlier, would take up an area totaling 9 sq.ms and provide a plot size of 5.78 sq.ms. The arable portion of this plot is a whopping 64%.

Even if you were to try and maximize the space used for the square garden beds the best percentage of arable land that you would get would still only be 36%, almost half that of the keyhole garden.

So, it makes complete sense to build these rather than waste valuable space constructing their square counterparts.

A common recipe for a successful keyhole garden is a ratio of 3:1 in the composition of brown and green material which forms the core garden and breaks down rapidly due to the heat generated by the natural decomposition

Possible Browns

Thin-layer brown materials such as:
Dry, yellow or brown leaves and brown
Grass dead, woody stalks or plants
•
Any paper and wood products: chopped
Twigs, shredded newspaper, phone books,
programs, a little slick paper is okay
•
sawdust
•
dryer lint, vacuum cleaner waste
•
Straw

-
wood ash from fireplaces (not a lot)
-
lots of cardboard
-
100% cotton, wool, or silk
Where to find browns:
-
Cardboard: furniture stores, appliance stores, hardware stores and some grocery stores.
-
Newspaper: ask at local newspaper offices, post office for phone books and junk mail (avoid plastics)

Possible Greens

Thin-layer green materials such as:
-
kitchen scraps from vegetables, melon rinds, eggshells, and fruit
-
coffee grounds and tea bags
-
freshly cut green leaves and grass clippings
-
manure
-
inexpensive bulk pet food
Where to find greens:
-

Coffee grounds with natural filters: coffee shops and restaurants.

•

Fresh manure (barnyard kind): landscape supply yards, horse stalls, or cow barns (avoid vet clinics

DON'T FORGET: Planning ahead for plant selection aids the decision of where your keyhole garden should be built (sun, rain, prevailing winds, house, shelter, etc.)

Yet another example of the concept is incredibly simple, slow, small solutions adding up to provide complexity, stability and abundance.

SWALES

Rain gardens are as old as agriculture especially in arid lands. For thousands of years, humans have harvested the water from rains too heavy to fully soak into the ground. A rain garden or catchment is a depression or basin on the surface of the soil where rainwater is collected from the surrounding landscape and can be used by plants in the basin. A depression may be man-made; however, many occur naturally. A man-made rain garden should be placed to optimize the capture of water from the immediate drainage area. Ditches or swales also may be used to divert water from other drainage areas. Water from a rooftop may be channeled through gutters and pipes to the rain garden.

A sloping hill in your backyard and a mattock and a hoe is an ideal place to set about fish scaling the landscape with swales.

A swale is a depression or ditch that follows the contour of the land like the lines used on topographical maps to illustrate elevation and gradient.

As with a rice terrace, when seen from above the line of the swale may curve across the surface of the land but when viewed edge on it will be perfectly horizontal and level allowing water to pool from end to end.

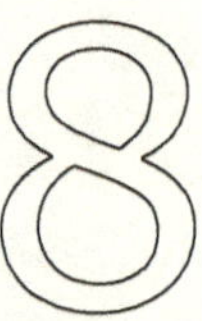

PERMACULTURE PERUSAL

Goji Berries

Growing Goji berries (also known as wolfberries) is a great option for introducing the "superfood" fruits into your garden. Now most would not call this plant as one to be thought of bugging out with it as a candidate. The Chinese railroad workers brought it with them as a primary cooking and fresh consumption mainstay and planted it all over the west everywhere the tracks led. I planted mine in places of honor in my keyhole gardens from KeyholeFarm.com as a permanent integral part of my garden.

If I ever had to bug out from Prepper Shack you can be assured the plants are going with me in some form or fashion. I have other Goji plantings on the property but these are new cuttings from a mother plant I bought off Ebay. Even though they are young I will still get berries this year. Goji Berry soup for health benefits and a better nutritional diet is part of my new regime of being ready to be my own health care provider no matter what.

I really like my commercial built keyhole

gardens, this is a small garden system, and vermiculture assures that I get maximum nutritional benefits from my crops as well being able to control the beds environment more closely. As an added benefit I also think of them as defensive barriers or an apocalyptic fighting position if one considers such necessary, because that much dirt can easily stop most any bullet fired into it.

The Lycium barbarum variety of Goji Berry Plants are a perennial in zones 3 to 10, they are actually quite remarkably heat and cold tolerant. Goji plants are also deciduous, which just means that they drop their leaves every year, usually once the first frost hits.

- **Protein:** Goji berries are one of the very few plant-based foods that can provide you with a complete protein. This means that the berries contain all of the amino acids, which are the building blocks of proteins that your body cannot make for itself. Meats and dairy products contain all of these essential amino acids, but most plants do not. Vegetarians and vegans typically combine foods like beans and grains to get a complete protein, but Goji berries can give you all of them in one package

- The Goji plant begins flowering in the second year with maximum fruit production in the 4th or 5th year.
- Goji (*Lycium barbarum*), a native of the Himalayan valleys of Tibet, has come to be known as wolfberry to some in the West and these berries aren't for everyone either — anyone who uses blood thinners or takes diabetic medication may have a negative reaction eating Goji berries, according to WebMD.

When in doubt, ask your doctor first. Goji berries can interfere with blood thinners like warfarin. If you take this medication, you should not eat the berries.

☐ Approximate **yield per plant:** Up to 6.7 pounds (3 kg) depending on climate
☐ Life **of plant:** Up to 90 years
☐ Companion **plants:**

- Companions: n/a
- Avoid: Avoid planting near potatoes and tomatoes

Vitamin E (very rarely found in fruits, usually only found in grains, seeds, and nuts.)

More protein than whole wheat (13% more), the Goji Berry displays an insulin-like action that is effective in fat decomposition.

Antioxidant-rich - According to Jodi Helmer, the author of *Goji Berries: Antioxidant Supreme*, goji berries are an excellent source of antioxidants such as polyphenols, flavonoids, carotenoids and vitamins A, C and E. In fact, the Goji berry contains approximately 500 times more vitamin C per weight than an orange and considerably more beta-carotene than carrots. These findings are reinforced by the Goji berries' high Oxygen Radical Absorbance Capacity (ORAC) score of 3,290, which shows that they contain much larger concentrations of antioxidants than most other fruits. Since antioxidants help neutralize the cell-damaging effects of free radicals, eating more antioxidant-rich foods like Goji berries can help guard us from degenerative diseases such as rheumatoid arthritis, Alzheimer's disease and most types of cancer.

High in nutrients - Though Goji berries are best-known for their antioxidant activity, they also contain an impressive number of vitamins and minerals. According to Paul Gross in his report, *The Top 20 Superfruits*, a quarter cup of Goji berries contains 11 essential vitamins and 22 trace minerals, including 24 percent of our RDI of potassium, 18 percent of our RDI of zinc and a whopping 100 percent of our RDI of iron, copper and riboflavin. They also contain 8 polysaccharides, a primary source of dietary fiber.

Fortify Liver

Goji berries contain a group of neutral chemical compounds called betaines which are the secret behind its long history of use to support liver health. Betaines have been shown to reduce fatty deposits in the liver which may result from any number of lifestyle factors (alcohol use, diabetes, diet, etc.) While controlled studies involving laboratory rats far outnumber those performed on humans, the history of the Goji berry speaks for itself.

Protection From UV Radiation

The juice derived from Goji berries can reduce the amount of damage done by ultraviolet radiation. According to a study published in January 2010 in "Photochemical and Photobiological Sciences," mice that consumed Goji berry juice had a significantly reduced inflammatory sunburn response to prolonged simulated ultraviolet radiation. Researchers believe that some of the antioxidants found in Goji berries are responsible for this protection, preventing the oxidative damage that would otherwise induce the inflammatory response. So consuming these while working in the garden under that hot sun just makes good sense.

Protection of Eye Health

While it is very difficult if not impossible to "fix" your eyes if you already have poor vision (short of having surgery), it is possible to protect your eyes from further damage using natural remedies. According to a study published in February 2011 in "Optometry and Vision Science," daily supplementation of Goji berries over the course of 90 days significantly aids in the prevention of soft drusen accumulation in the eyes of elderly patients, an early warning sign of age-related macular degeneration. This exact mechanism behind this effect is currently unclear. Taurine, a compound found in Goji berries, is also beneficial in slowing the development of eye conditions related to diabetes.

Goji berries contain two key nutrients that support vision: lutein and zeaxanthin. Studies show that consuming high amounts of lutein and zeaxanthin lowers the risk for developing age-related macular degeneration, cataracts, and other eye diseases. So, what all this means, is that you are growing your own cheaper and better form of eye vitamins!

Prevent vision loss - Goji berries contain high concentrations of the carotenoid zeaxanthin which has been recognized for its ability to protect eyes from damage caused by oxidation and for reducing the risk of age-related macular degeneration (AMD) which is the number one cause of blindness in human beings over the age of 65. Hopefully, we all plan on making it to age 65 and knowing the risks that are indicated in this study, doesn't it make good sense to be including this in our diet now instead of finding out we should have been doing it later?

Studies have also been performed regarding the polysaccharides in Goji berries and how they may reduce or prevent damage to the retina and optic nerve.

According to a study published in the 2005 issue of the *British Journal of Nutrition*, Goji_berries contain properties that prevent the risk of vision loss. Researchers at *Hong Kong Polytechnic University* fed 14 healthy volunteers a serving of 15 grams of Goji berries daily for 28 days while comparing their blood levels to 13 control volunteers. After 28 days, the volunteers who consumed the fruits experienced significantly raised zeaxanthin levels in the blood (zeaxanthin is an antioxidant present in Goji berries that helps preserve eyesight). Therefore, if you're suffering from poor or deteriorating eyesight, consider adding more Goji berries to your diet.

Blood-glucose Regulation

Goji berries are one of a handful of fruits that can be safely enjoyed by diabetics. With a GI value of only 29 (less than 40 is considered low) Goji berries won't cause a spike in blood-glucose levels like some fruits. There have also been studies which show that Goji berries may have a positive impact on reducing insulin resistance. Regular ingestion of Goji berries can also promote healthy weight, triglyceride, and cholesterol levels.

Heart disease: Consuming Goji berries has been shown to increase the amount of an enzyme in the human body called superoxide dismutase. This is the enzyme that prevents cholesterol from oxidizing. In its oxidized form, cholesterol is harmful to your heart and contributes to heart disease. By eating more Goji berries you can lower your risk of dangerous heart conditions.

Defend Your Brain Preppers

Possibly due to its high levels of calcium and B vitamins, Goji berries have also been shown to protect the mind against degenerative disorders like Alzheimer's disease. In fact, its ability to defend the nervous system is one of the few health benefits of this amazing "superfruit" that has been scientifically researched and confirmed to be effective on humans. So if you're having trouble with memory, mental clarity, or any other neurological functions, you just might benefit from a handful of dried Goji berries mixed in with your morning cereal or smoothie. You might also ask yourself in a starvation on the horizon environment of living long-term in a bug out situation that you may expect such mental afflictions and be planning accordingly. Do you see why I list Goji Berries in this book now?

Anti-Aging

Longevity and anti-aging properties: The fruits of the Goji plant have long been associated in China with longevity. Modern research has found that certain oils in the berries, called sesquiterpinoids can increase your production of human growth hormone. No other plant has been shown to have such an effect on these hormones. As you age, your production of this hormone decreases. By consuming the berries, you can up the production and may see the anti-aging effects in your appearance and overall health. Goji berries are full of antioxidants that help to protect DNA from damage caused by free-radicals – the biological waste byproducts that our bodies naturally produce simply by living. Goji berries also contain useful amino acids and minerals that aid our bodies in the process of repairing and regenerating cells. What this means is that a daily serving of Goji berries or Goji juice can actually help to slow or in some cases even reverse the signs of aging.

Fortify Immune System

Goji berries have traditionally been used to fortify the immune system against infection and recent studies have given us probable cause to believe it works. Carotenoid beta-carotene and amino-acid Cystine found in Goji berries are both recognized for their positive impact on immune function. Goji berries also contain zinc which is crucial for immune health and one of the most widely-used remedies for the prevention of otherwise incurable viral illnesses such as the common cold. Furthermore, the polysaccharides contained in Goji berries have been shown to stimulate increased immune function.

Cancer-Fighting Properties

Small, fleshy berries like the Goji berry contain antioxidant compounds known as polyphenols that could protect against the development of cancer. These antioxidants fight against, diminish and repair cell damage that results from inflammation and oxidative stress from free radicals, preventing the likelihood of cancerous tumor development. Antioxidants like those in Goji berries may also improve the effectiveness of chemotherapy by weakening tumor cells, reports a study published in 2008 in the "Journal of Agricultural and Food Chemistry."

Benefits of Goji (cancer)

The chemical component that gives Goji this positive effect is beta-sitosterol (also called cinchol. This compound is found in the bright red berries themselves and beta-sitosterol can affectively decrease the size of overgrown cells; In fact it can even induce apoptosis (cell suicide) of tumor cells. Apoptosis is a process during which the body induces cell suicide for dysfunctional or abnormal cells which can potentially cause harm to the body if their replication continues.

This property of Goji berries makes it a more commonly used treatment for prostate enlargement. After men reach their 40s, the cells of the prostate gland enlarge to a certain extent. When it persists it can develop into a condition called benign prostatic hyperplasia (BPH). If left unaddressed the enlargement of this gland can cause obstruction of the urinary tract thus making urination difficult and, in some instances, painful for older men. In the case of prostate cancer, these cells enlarge and divide out of control causing them to damage normal cells tissues surrounding these abnormal cells. And this can do extensive damage to normal body functioning. Because the beta-sitosterol in Goji effectively reduces the size of these swollen cells without serious side affects it is becoming used commonly by physicians. It is used as a precautionary treatment but in patients with cancers, it can be used along with other medications to assist in the reduction of tumor cells (no known drug interactions have been documented for beta-sitosterol).

Improved Feelings of Well-being

If vitality is your aim, this is your berry. According to a study published in May 2008 in the "Journal of Alternative and Complementary Medicine," drinking juice derived from Goji berries has a positive effect on overall well-being. In a SHTF situation or for that matter in everyday life I think we can all benefit as well as know others that need this plant in their diets. Study participants drank Goji berry juice daily for a period of 15 days, reporting perceived levels of energy, quality of sleep and feelings of happiness. After 15 days, both the Goji berry group and the placebo group reported higher levels of happiness, but the Goji berry group also reported improved energy levels, lower fatigue, and lower stress and improved digestive function. While these measures are subjective, the findings are statistically significant for mine as well as your consideration and further research in dealing with disaster related Post Traumatic stress (PTSD) syndrome. Because they contain such a wide variety of vitamins, minerals, amino-acids, and oils that have a positive impact on hormone production and overall health of the human body, it's no wonder that science has proven that Goji berries just make you feel good. In a post apocalyptic world or when a tornado just took your barn down, you want to feel better and get over it right without relying on alcohol or other substances to numb the blow right?

Improve male fertility - Goji berries have long been considered a male aphrodisiac in China, and more studies are starting to confirm these allegations. According to a Chinese study published in the July 2006 issue of *Life Sciences*, for example, rats that were fed Goji berries maintained testicular function when subjected to heat. The researchers also found that certain constituents in Goji berries regulated the release of sexual hormones, boosted hormone levels and improved the quality and quantity of sperm in male rats. Ok, all you lab rats living after a major disaster, are we going to repopulate the world or just get happy trying?

How to Grow Goji Berry Plants

Once established, Goji berries are incredibly easy to grow. They'll grow in almost any type of soil, and can even thrive in poor soil, as they are used to the mountainous regions in the Himalayas. They are reasonably drought-tolerant, and will even grow in partial shade (though you'll get more berries from them if you grow them in full sun). Once established Goji berry plants are easy to grow and maintain. They can grow in almost any soil type, light-sandy, medium-loamy, heavy-clay or any combination of the three. Even soils of poor soil structure and nutrient content will grow Goji plants, but soils of better quality will allow for better flowering and fruiting characteristics. Are you all following me with the bug in bug out aspect of having a highly documented beneficial plant that you have access now to replacing that pharmaceutical crap that will not be available come grid down or healthcare insurance loss? A well drained soil is a must as Goji berry plants will not grow well in wet or soggy conditions. Goji plants have an aggressive root system and are quite drought tolerant after they are established.

Goji Berry plants are very adaptable, but for the very best results, test your soil, and then adjust the pH to between 6.8 – 8.1 if you are able. You can add lime to raise the pH if necessary or aluminum_sulfate to lower it, other instructions for sweetening your soil or adding acid is included in this book.

Flowers

The Goji berry grows into a large shrub reaching heights of 7-10 feet with vines that can reach 10 feet. After two years the bushes will start to fruit, and from four years you'll start to get very heavy yields. In early summer the bushes will produce small, delicate, trumpet-shaped flowers that will be either white or purple. Both colored flowers can feature on one plant, so they provide visual interest before the berry production begins.

The berries will begin to set in autumn. The ripe fruit are sweet and juicy and almost shiny in appearance. The flowers will continue to bloom right up until the first frosts, however, so your plants will be red, white and purple throughout late summer and autumn.

They are beautiful to have in your garden, delicious, nutritious, and cheap and easy to grow. If you want health-boosting berries on tap you should consider investing in a Goji berry bush or two.

GROW GOJI BERRY PLANTS IN CONTAINERS

Goji Berry plants can easily be grown in containers on your deck or patio. Goji plant roots like to grow deep, but the plant itself will stop growing once the roots touch the bottom of the container, so they won't grow as large as the plants grow in the ground. One advantage is that you may very well see Goji berries in the first or second season, rather than the third, which is normally the case when they are grown in the ground.

So you've received your bare root plants. They will survive for awhile without being planted, but we recommend that you plant them as soon as possible. We also suggest that you get them established inside, in a sunny location, before moving them outside, also to a sunny location. Your Goji plant will appreciate some afternoon shade if you live in a very hot climate (Temps above 100°F).

- Place the bare root plants in a jar or container with room-temperature water and allow them to soak for about 15-minutes.
- Prepare your container. We recommend a container at least as deep as a five-gallon bucket, but it does not have to be wide. Your container or pot should have drainage holes in the bottom (if it doesn't—make some), so

you may also want to provide a drain pan for the container to sit in.

- Mix about 1/3 sand to 2/3 soil in order to provide the best growing medium and drainage, though any good potting soil will work. In hot, dry areas, we recommend <u>Ultimate Container Mix</u>. Fill the container, leaving 2 to 3-inches at the top.
- Dig a hole in the middle of the container a couple of inches deeper than to the crown of the plant (where the roots meet the stem), pushing loose soil back in until with the roots lightly resting on the soil in the hole, the crown is level with the top of the soil.
- Push the soil back in, filling around the roots and up to the crown, gently tamping as you go.
- Water well and push more soil around the plant if necessary, watering again to let the soil settle.
- You should continue to keep your Goji plant moist, but not overly wet, until you see new growth sprouting, usually in about 2-weeks.
- Apply an inch or two of mulch in order to help with moisture retention (and because it looks nice). If you mulch, you will depend upon touch to check soil moisture, or water into a large reservoir under the planter so it is wicked from the bottom up.

You may see flowers, after which fruit will follow, the first season, depending upon when you plant; but more than likely it will be the second season. Remember that containerized plants will feel the heat and cold more because their roots are in soil above the ground. Be weather-aware, providing adequate moisture when it is extremely hot and dry, as containerized plants will usually dry out quicker and in order to provide protection for your plant if the temperatures become really cold.

GROW GOJI BERRY PLANTS IN THE GROUND

You can grow Goji Berry plants in the ground in any relatively sunny location, as long as you have room for expansion. Adult Goji plants can grow up to 8-feet high and wide, though some gardeners prune their Goji plants to keep them within a desired size range. You can even grow Goji bushes as a hedge or you can train them to a trellis, in which case, they can get as tall as 10-feet.

To make this really simple and to give your Goji Berry Plant the best start, we recommend that you start it in a container, though you don't need a 5-gallon size. In fact, you can buy a 4 to 6-inch peat pot and not even have to worry about taking it back out of the pot to transplant it. This will greatly reduce the stress involved with transplanting; further ensuring your Goji plant will thrive. If you are starting it in a container, you just follow steps 1 through 7 above, at which point you can transplant your Goji plant into the ground. Goji plants growing in the ground will sometimes start to produce fruit the second season, but will not go into full production until the third year.

If you are putting it directly into the ground:

- Choose a sunny site if you live anywhere *but* in the desert southwest, where you will either want to have shade or be able to put up a shade cloth during the hottest part of the day.
- Follow step 1 above, and then prepare your soil, testing and amending it if needed.
- Skip to step 4, and continue through step 8 above, applying mulch immediately, rather than waiting, and carefully monitoring soil moisture. It is critical that it not be allowed to dry out until you see new growth start to sprout, usually in about two weeks.

How many plants should I plant?

A 30 foot row with 15 plants has the potential to produce up to 100 pounds of berries per year, which would supply about 80% of a person's annual nutrient needs. Three ounces of dried berries have approximately 80% of a person's daily nutrient requirements (not calories). So you're not going to be living off the Goji but you will not be worrying about your loss of access to vitamin supplements grid down or economically challenged.

PRUNING YOUR GOJI BERRY PLANTS

Pruning is normally done in the winter, but they can also be gently trimmed throughout the season to shape the canopy and to improve berry yield.

You will not want to prune them heavily the first year. Identify the largest, healthy shoot, which will be the main trunk. Gradually remove the lower lateral shoots, with the goal in mind of keeping the trunk clear for the first 15-inches, and then when your Goji plant reaches 24-inches , remove the growing tip in order to stimulate the growth of additional side branches.

Your Goji will grow and thrive, even if you never prune it once. However, it will be easier to harvest with some selective pruning. Simply shorten the horizontal branches by about half to two-thirds in early spring, just as the buds begin to break. Plants can withstand severe pruning, but fruiting may be minimal in the following season. To prune adult plants, you just remove the branches above the height that you wish to keep. You should maintain clearance from the ground up to about 15-inches. You can also identify any ineffective branches. These usually grow very fast, straight and smooth and will not be very productive, so if they aren't essential to the overall look, they can simply be removed. Remember that Goji Berry plants grow similar to a weeping willow. If allowed to grow un-pruned you can end up with a mighty ugly plant, though "ugly" is only in the eye of the beholder, and you may thoroughly enjoy this natural look. You should always prune the plant after a heavy berry season as berries are produced on new growth only.

Drying Goji berries is a great way to store berries that aren't eaten fresh. You can add these to cereals or salads and make them into tea.

To dry them...

1. Spread your Goji berries on a baking sheet making sure they are not touching
2. Set the oven to its lowest temperature and leave the door slightly open
3. Bake the berries for up to 12 hours until they have dried
4. Allow them to cool
5. Store in an airtight jar

Berries stored in this way can last up to a year.

☐ **Storage life (dried)**: up to one year if dried but NOT refrigerated

☐ **Storage life (dried and refrigerated)**: up to two years if dried and refrigerated

PESTS- Other than attracting birds and other animals, Goji berries are very pest- and disease-resistant. This makes them a very low maintenance plant. As mentioned previously, do not plant them near potatoes or tomatoes as this may result in blight-type diseases.

Artichoke: These thistle relatives, properly called globe artichokes, aren't the most soft and cuddly vegetables, but yield a large tasty flower bud. Growing artichokes does take a bit of room in the garden, as they can grow to 6 feet or more in height, and like most perennial vegetables, a couple of years of growth is often necessary before they've matured to the point that you can harvest enough flowers to grace your table. While they can be started from seed, artichokes can also be planted from dividing an established patch, or from starter plants that may be available from the garden center.

Collards: Most people don't get too excited when they hear that collard greens are for dinner, but few people know that these greens have been ranked as one of the most nutritionally dense foods in existence. In the ANDI score rating, which stand for aggregate nutritional density index, collard greens have been given a score of 1000 out of 1000. The leaves of this plant are literally packed with energy of Mother Nature. They contain more protein by weight than beef.

Tree collards another species usually found in California but gaining in popularity everywhere are also an excellent source of vitamins K, A, C, folate, manganese and calcium. Their high concentration of fiber means they'll keep you regular too. Tree collards can be eaten any way that regular collard greens can be eaten, as a wrap for a raw burrito, sautéed with other vegetables, or as a raw green juice.

To grow tree collards, you'll need to get a plant from a friend or nursery. There are two

varieties available, white veined and purple veined.
(Either is great.)

.Other great things to grow

Kale Winterbore and walking stick kale

Think about growing sugar cane

There are a Lot of edible flowers

BASIC CURES FOR BASIC AILMENTS

IT IS NOT WHAT YOU'RE THINKING!

Remember I told you that you could take what you learned here anywhere with you and survive?

I excerpted this out of my book Bug Out Gardening because I think it is good enough to be shared again and repeated here as applied to the backyard scenario as well. I apologize to those that have already read it but it was needed to complete this book.
I NO LONGER SELL THESE SEED PACKETS YOU WILL HAVE TO MAKE YOUR OWN!

BASIC CURES FOR BASIC AILMENTS

THE DISASTER PLASTER

The amazing throw and grow solution for day one grid down worries and anxieties.

RON FOSTER`S DISASTER PLASTER

A weed is a plant that has mastered every survival skill except learning how to grow in rows. ~ Doug Larsen Be a weed.

Thinking about how things were often referred to back in the day, I remember that folks used to call some medical remedies a plaster. Now depending on its use or the healing intentions of a plaster, this word can mean several different things; it also varies by locale or custom. It can be used as an old fashioned word for a Band-Aid for example or a remedy like what usually comes to many people's mind is the old fashioned mustard plaster they would stick on your chest for bad colds or flu.

BASIC CURES FOR BASIC AILMENTS

Anyway one way of dealing with a mishap or trying to deal with a disaster is to put a temporary or permanent patch on it. A plaster if you would. Having such a remedy on hand for the conditions one may find themselves in a bug out location without an already prepared garden can be the difference of you making it or not making it so I would strongly advise you to consider adding one of my personally designed seed selection plasters to your B.O.B. gear if survival gardening is part of your disaster preparations or intentions.

I came up with the notion or my carefully crafted concept of what I now call my original copyrighted "Disaster Plaster" survival planting method using common wild edibles when I looked over my small heavily wooded 3 acre property and the thirteen 10x4 foot raised beds in my garden and asked myself the question "what would I do gardening wise different from what I am doing now if the shit had just hit the fan?" How would I greatly increase my yields?

My answer like most people I know who are "Bug In" prepared type preppers or part-time homesteaders who are planning on staying wherever they are during and after a grid down mega disaster for a long period of time, will answer "Plant Like Hell!" Till up any bit of extra cleared land I can and sow about all the seed I have on hand except for my reserves!"

BASIC CURES FOR BASIC AILMENTS

Go crazy wondering to myself if all those old seeds I have been hanging on to just in case of such an event might sprout or am I just wasting space and time fooling with them?

Germination rates on those things would be impossible to guess but I guess they are a measure of hope in some way. Be glad that I had some backup seeds stored in nitrogen even if the varieties were not what I was used to growing.

Go crazy like the Chinese do in a famine and plant corn right up to the telephone poles! Start raking the hell out of leaves in my woods and doing the big compost pile I never got around to. Slash and burn where I can by imitating the time honored but very destructive gardening practices of the indigenous peoples of the rain forests in South America and various geographic areas of Africa. Wait a minute now I am getting carried away. Now what is the first and best thing I can do to insure my success and get a gauge on my seed viability and germination rates?

I will finally get around to building that emergency green house I have had in back of my mind with some tree limbs I got using that roll of clear plastic I have saved just for this occasion in my prep shed.

BASIC CURES FOR BASIC AILMENTS

Then I need to go round up all the empty spare containers I have like left over like nursery six packs and gallon containers, foil roasting pans, egg crates, you name it and fill them with soil and start seedlings! They can start growing long before I get my newly cleared ground ready to plant with seeds and be back up or more controlled growing condition transplants,. That's the ticket! I got my plan coming together now. But something just does not seem right? What might that be?

"Oh hell!" I exclaim to myself. "Dirt, where the hell am I going to get dirt to fill those empty containers? I only have about one 50lb bag of potting soil and part of another left. Now readers please note I grow about 90% organic around here at Prepper Shack but the soil I am on is pitiful and if you are not raised bed gardening it you can't grow anything but a blister at all unless you add some fertilizer of some sort.

The soil is played out terrace farmland that nature took back with forest but its maybe only a ¼ of an inch of topsoil, red dirt, sand and then hard clay. The land actually slides if you disturb it and try to make a bed. I have 2 bags (50lb each) of 10-10-10 on hand as part of my preps and also use it to fertilize my fruit trees, berry and nut bushes. That is the cheapest most efficient way I can attempt the task.

I use a small military pick shovel to dig with every early spring before they put leaves out to

BASIC CURES FOR BASIC AILMENTS

amend the soil so they stand half a chance to grow and by that I mean it quite literally. I permacultured the devil out of this place when I first got here and continue to try to add to it. Bug In gardening anyone?

Well money was short and dreams were big so I got dozens of fruit and nut tree seedlings off ebay as sets which averaged about 7-9 inches tall and planted them with a handful of potting mix and the soil from the hole they were being planted in and forgot about them for a few yrs while I tried to keep 10 good 6ft or better trees alive that I had purchased for about 20 bucks a pop. Two and a half years later my bigger orchard trees are producing fruit but not as much as they could. Maybe because those commercial fruit tree food spikes are so expensive and if a tree was supposed to get three or more I only gave them one and now with my economics being stressed again once more I couldn't afford that. I just pick axe a hole and fill with fertilizer to amend.

Yes I can be considered a poor man but an adaptable and honest one, and yes I could of done some crazy do it yourself organics to help all my trees along, but life and laziness said no that wasn't happening.

I also have the philosophy that when it comes to permaculture on my land that I plant something and let nature and it decide if it thrives

BASIC CURES FOR BASIC AILMENTS

or dies while I become a bystander and observe and research what does well or doesn't through my "set it and forget it "land conservatory practices I am wont to do to find out what type of flora and fauna grows best on this peculiar soil, I have naturally and without much care or intervention on my part.

Digging up a bunch of dirt off the property to fill all those containers can be done but it would be a laborious pain in the butt that may or may not grow something. I know that yellow squash will get about 5 inches tall and blossom and die planting directly in it from dry land farming experiments outside the normal soil amended kitchen garden. But now is a good time to admit planting Seminole squash on the edge of the orchard grew without any help by me and if I attended it marginally with some weeding and fertilization my success would have been better.

Anyway I know my land and what is needed to be added where and why on it. One little section of your land is not the same as everywhere else on the same property. I originally planned before contemplating and then writing this book to pretty much go bat crap crazy on day one of a known long term grid down situation evaluating how I could expand my growing area, to maximize my yield by adding more labor intensive but organically sound growing practices on my forlorn dejected and unmanaged guerilla gardening

BASIC CURES FOR BASIC AILMENTS

survival planting plots to minimize my insect and disease risks using every primitive and modern trick of gardening I knew in hopes of success.

You see I have been curiously screwing around and doing hands on research for over thirty five years of taking everything from a shovel to a tiller to a patch of uncleared ground and planting things and observing the results be they good or poor. I have learned the majority of soils I have encountered both on properties I have owned and on friends generally will not produce vegetables without some kind of soil amendment.

Hence, having a good balanced fertilizer on hand like a bag of slow release 8/8/8 etc is essential if you don't have organic materials like manure to build your soil. I also keep some on hand if something needed side dressing to increase yields or combat problems because of deficiencies in a new bed I am building up. Although I don't like chemical fertilizers and prefer organic gardening methods, in a grid down hit it and get it situation you are a dang fool if you haven't already gone out and spent about $15 for a 50lb bag of good commercial agricultural grade fertilizer while it is cheap and available. You can always trade it or get a neighbors garden started in the worst of dirt, its called survival, right? No time then to get picky about whether something is organic or not when the wolf is howling at your door.

BASIC CURES FOR BASIC AILMENTS

That being said, I started to wonder. Doing all that commercial or homemade fertilizer style gardening is what I originally had set out to explain how to do and what I would do myself to expand my organic garden or have a means of growing if I had to bug out personally.

Except for some elaborating on this theme and adding some homemade organic fertilizers that you could make in the field I figured I would have covered the subject of bug out gardening sufficiently but I felt compelled. That's right I said compelled to stop spending so much time on that subject and instead tell you something that is pretty dang profound and a way to starvation proof yourself.

Did you know that there are 13 edible plants that are found everywhere on the planet? That's right! I can go from Alabama to Alaska to Finland to Jordan to Australia and find one or many more of these species of plants growing. I can find them in the inner cities; I can find them in the suburbs or on a barren road median. The means of mine and your survival is basically nothing more than eating the weeds!

Yea I know, everyone knows that there is an abundance of food in backyards and roadsides but those botanical field guides are confusing and hard to read to let alone memorize right? You want to have this knowledge, you have an identification

BASIC CURES FOR BASIC AILMENTS

guide of North American plants maybe you occasionally look at and try to remember and take to the field for some practical hands on learning.

There will be time for all that later you shrug and take some small comfort in having it in your preps and can't wait to attend a meeting with a decent naturalist to point some things out in the woods on a hike at some event you plan on attending. You watch YouTube videos and sometimes force yourself to listen to just about anybody occasionally to pick up some information on whatever plant you decided you were driven into investigating but that whole wild crafting, herb gathering plant identification thing has got you still real hazy about it all and there is just not enough time to learn everything now, right?

Well I would say a lot of us have approached the art of finding some pot greens all wrong. We spend so much time looking for some obscure plant or deciphering scientific texts we don't look right under our feet for a solution.

Do you know who is probably the best naturalist or wild food gatherer you got in your neighborhood? That old man or women up the road who is constantly out doing some gardening and digging up weeds. Most of them don't even know they have the master's eye for identifying edible plants. They will tell you they see weeds, what type of weed it is, its growth habits, how hard it is

BASIC CURES FOR BASIC AILMENTS

to eradicate it, what it means your soil is lacking in nutrients that the presence of the weed indicates, what is the best natural or chemical way to kill it, etc. but like I said most don't know that pesky weed can be what's for dinner.

The other guy or gal on your block that you might seek out who knows a bunch about the weeds in your neighborhood or state is one of those chemical lawn guys you can bug for identification with mixed results.

A lot of them get educated in identification of noxious weeds and their control, but on the same note a lot more time is often spent on memorizing what the chemical is that gets rid of pretty much everything and how to sell you a contract so they can spray that crap all over your lawn and house stairs.

Misaligned weeds like the dandelion are waged war upon in every neighborhood but somehow or the other they persist somewhere else.

See you already know one edible plant very well, Dandelions! The whole plant is edible. Oh yuck! You might cry remembering some uninformed common childhood warnings, that white sap in them is poisonous! No its not, you can play the dandelion flute if you want! So now knowing that and maybe looking up some further

BASIC CURES FOR BASIC AILMENTS

facts that you can use the roots to make a bitter tasting coffee substitute you begin looking on this lowly weed a bit different. You find it has tangible value as a survival food procurement skill. Something that you are confident will increase your chances of survivability that is easy to spot confidently by you when present.

I got to thinking about how blessed I was to have my little piece of land that I am hopefully going to be living out my life on and have had the chance to experiment on and try building up my garden soil organically every year and pondered my original hypothecation of "How does one explain how to build a bug out garden?" and concluded one does not focus on that aspect.

I fight with the weeds on my property all the time by hand or mechanical means because I wish to increase my vegetable production but you might say I have been blessed because I ain't sweating having them edible weeds around.

The reason being is that if I had crop failure caused by drought, insects, disease etc. at least one of those darn weeds I have been wrestling with would grow in profusion from my neglect and mother nature's nurturing and I would be eating greens and tubers anyway if I was forced by circumstance or just plain wanted to for nutrition or health.

BASIC CURES FOR BASIC AILMENTS

I know a lot of my weeds in my gardens walkways and I know that which are edible and or medicinal, I also know that many are mostly better for me to be eating than the more tasty and more demanding veggies I normally consume or grow. Nature is a great gardener; she beats me to the punch every spring and already has her wild plants out in spring with tender shoots ready for me to eat before I even put the first shovel to the ground to plant a seed. There is pretty much something out there in the garden to eat long after I say I am done for the summer or decide I don't want to do a winter garden again this year.

This concept got me to thinking and rethinking about what would I do if the poo had hit the fan and I had to abandon my farmstead and bug out with nothing more than an entrenching tool and selection of so called survival seeds.

What skill set do I need to share or hone myself to accomplish this task? I have a decided advantage in surviving through wild plant identification but that is only from mostly studying those 13 plants that occur everywhere that a whole lot of folks don't have a clue about. I could research and list attributes for those buying farmland about what the weeds on it said about soil quality but that could be an injustice.

I had 25 acres one time that had at one time been a hog farm. The guy had planted acres of

BASIC CURES FOR BASIC AILMENTS

purslane on it and after discing it in and tilling and planting cover crops etc it still plagued me and my garden. Purslane is called pigweed because lots of people planted this stuff for the hogs to root up and eat.

In an "I want to just be farming regular herbs and vegetable world" purslane is a scourge and noxious weed, in a SHTF world it is my most prolific and nutritious reliable food source, my medicine, my untended bounty. It's rare to find an entire field full of it but I have never seen a field without it and in profusion. They herbicide the hell out of the side of a lot of roads but it persistently still springs up. I would rather not eat it from such areas but no telling how long after it was wiped out it was brought back in again from the wind or birds and animals to grow anew.

If I had to just pick a bug out location wouldn't it be cool if I started with an abandoned farm field that had lots of weeds growing in it? Better yet, some of the tastier weeds growing in proliferation? Yea, that is what I am going to do when I am out and about, start spying for and paying attention to places with an abundance of edible weeds. Hell, if I was able I would sink my bug out garden right down in the center of a good weed patch after I had gathered the edibles for that day's dinner and tomorrow's fertilizer and bug in and start gardening!

BASIC CURES FOR BASIC AILMENTS

I know fighting with the weeds will be a daily chore for awhile but at least I can eat what I am weeding and waiting for a more civilized vegetable to grow. That's another thing about these thirteen weeds, they follow along growing where ever man has settled and dwelt. We kind of have a symbiotic relationship with them you might say. That is if we can understand and recognize them for what they are, then we have a survival garden often times already provided by mother nature, but man likes to play with his environment and regional tastes. Likes and dislikes eradicate this survival garden in order to provide for lawns or big agricultural fields that change the landscape.

I continued to challenge myself with the question of what should I do day one of a disaster and examined what it was that I wanted most from my desperate disaster gardening plans and came up with simply more edible weeds!

They require no extra fertilizer, are drought and pest resistant and seem to be pretty much a carefree survival solution. All I have to do is encourage the species I prefer and continue to discourage those I don't.

Instead of tilling up and breaking a lot of sweat working more land while burning more calories I can't afford with the impending food shortage gearing up, while expending my precious little bit of extra gas in my preps I have stored and

BASIC CURES FOR BASIC AILMENTS

diminishing other irreplaceable resources trying to force the land to grow my more recognizable vegetables, why don't I try expending minimal effort working with mother nature instead of working so hard against her? I already know she has the upper hand and usually wins in the end.

If I want more forgeable dandelions to be growing on that strip of unused land in front of my street that only occasionally gets mowed due to my freedom of living on a dead end country road, then I figure if the lights go out for months or years why not throw a bunch of dandelions seeds out on it instead of trying to think what might grow out there with the few seeds I got left from planting everywhere else?

For that matter if I was forced to bug out somewhere and start anew well then I know I would wish I had me a bunch of dandelion and other weed seeds to jump start any empty plot of land I had access to. That is when it dawned on me to make such a seed grenade. Eureka! Oh a commercially packaged conglomeration of wildflower seeds exists as well as those that grow grass from those grow it anywhere lawn patches but no one to my knowledge has ever come up with a proprietary blend of edible weed seeds to tip natures scales in their favor and thus my invention of the "Disaster Plaster" was born!

BASIC CURES FOR BASIC AILMENTS

I had come up with a simple and cost effective means to insure my survival and others that had been eluding me even after my many years studying emergency management and practicing my prepping and homesteading.

Not just any weed seeds would do and not just any seed company would be the one I chose to private label or co-pack for me. Being astute in the private label business as well as being networked into the commercial seeds men servicing the prepper community and backyard gardeners, I made contact and through much deliberation and resourcing came up with an offering for "Disaster Plasters" that I am proud to present to you for your purchasing consideration. You could assemble your own or maybe even do some wild crafting and get some seeds for free but if you want a ready made solution with high germination rates and the proper species mix, please try mine. You can find my seed selections at Kingsmountainseeds.webs.com.

A word of caution is in order regarding what a lot of people and some governments and agencies consider to be noxious weeds. Handle with them care and in some states you will find certain laws apply so please make yourself aware of any local restrictions that might apply to your area. In other words don't get stupid and try growing your entire backyard in edible weeds etc. unless it is truly a dire emergency that needs a

BASIC CURES FOR BASIC AILMENTS

plaster on that disaster. Your neighbors will thank you and so will I.

Personally I don't want one single seed of the blends I have managed to put together to touch my soil or fall upon my carpet for that matter. I often joke that I feel like I need to put on a hazmat suit and enter a clean chamber every time I mess with making up a packet of my insta-weed throw and grow. I treat them with due respect because to not treat them so is to invite a possible disaster.

I am country boy homesteading, dirt digging farmsteading prepper playing hobbyist with all kinds of rare vegetables and herbs while attempting to grow the biggest organic tomato in the county for bragging rights and less weeds means less work and more satisfaction as well as success.

A bunch of extra weeds could spell failure to some of my less tended vegetable and rare plant plots or permaculture endeavors if I get a bunch of newly introduced voracious growing weeds to contend with. I got enough weeds of my own without purposely or accidentally introducing a new host of others, but after close study of a disastrous grid down, humanity ending, societal collapsing, dire survival situation that I recognize as a possible threat or risk, I opt to have on hand my nemesis all prepackaged and ready to go. Famine may visit

BASIC CURES FOR BASIC AILMENTS

but starvation won't be able to take purchase at my door as long as I have access to edible weeds.

While you can pretty much guarantee most likely that everyone from prepper to farmer to sheeple is busy freaking out on just what they are going to do next come apocalyptic grid down, I have my own iron clad preparedness plan and it is I am happy to say as fool proof as Mother Nature herself in my opinion. Nothing is fool proof in this or any other world as we are all unfortunately well aware of but when it gets down to trusting dumb luck and seeds that don't seem to mind finding their own way to a sidewalk crack in a big city and growing and thriving regardless of conditions then I say that my plan is looking pretty good about now.

For those of you not adept at plant identification, it will be a saving grace to you to have on hand this book in printed format (or write down the fertilizer recipes if you just have electronic versions available) and a "Disaster Plaster" because hands on education in identification comes with that insurance policy in the form of wild edible food. You will soon be able to identify and recognize many forms of edible weeds in their various stages of life by seeing and doing. These skills will serve you well and expand your newly found survival skill expanded foraging territories that include pretty much most anywhere you might be walking around at someday.

BASIC CURES FOR BASIC AILMENTS

By reducing my traditional gardening methods through using this back to the land human assisted innovation, I now have lots of time to get my indoor preps in further order. Oh, I still have a few chores I need to do increasing my truck garden type vegetable production here and there but mostly it will be business as usual except grabbing a couple of tea bags full of weed seeds and doing the sprinkle the seed shuffle here and there on some of those places I have identified as having potential for an edible weed crop and go back inside to wait this calamity out.

The property will fast go looking unattended and overgrown, faster than the few weekly mowed plots around me anyway that will now probably sound like every tiller in America just cranked up all at once soon as the survival seed packages finally get used if folks got them with mixed results.

Oh the music of my tillers engine will also join the fray as that plot of soil I was going to eventually turn into a garden gets a lick and a promise with the addition of some commercial fertilizer and maybe some topsoil but I will be done with that and planting in a day.

Sprinkling my little Disaster Plasters on the soil with trepidation and a smile works wonders for my soul because I know that if I got everything

BASIC CURES FOR BASIC AILMENTS

wrong about today and planting a new garden I will still have accomplished an amazing feat.

I said with confidence, Mother Nature please feed me and provide for my needs and for others and I am 100% sure she shall. Weeds excel at being in survival mode, that's what they do best and they do it best by not having anyone but the wind and the rain helping them along.

No fertilizer and no tilling. Well, we might count some of those sidewalk crack growing weeds taking advantage of a rich limestone environment from the concrete but no one planted them there or try to mimic it as a gardening method although someday in a chaotic future I can imagine Mother Nature having a field day breaking up concrete with ever persistent growth of plants that will no longer be trod upon daily by humans as nature retakes her domains.

If I was forced to bug out I would certainly heed my own advice on a bug out vegetable garden but I wouldn't be waiting for it to produce to feed me in 60-90 days. No I would improve upon my situation first by upping the ante that I would be able to find shortly for myself an augmentation to the roots and herbs I was dependant on for daily survival until a crop came in by selectively salting the ground with food producing perennials that did not require my

BASIC CURES FOR BASIC AILMENTS

further attention after throwing them to the wind upon their appointed places.

My now newly weed enhanced and overgrown land areas that would give horrors to herbicide companies and my pocket book to try and control is now well managed by me using nothing more than my desire to eat and graze upon its abundance. I eat it, I tear it out by roots to consume it or make tea and it decides that loose soil is a perfect place to establish new growth or introduces a new weed I would be less likely to consume but has other amazing attributes I can study.

My formula for the ideal disaster plaster to put on my land can vary by local soil types, seasons and weather but rather than just customize for my own needs its easier and more beneficial to choose what mix of seeds works best for me universally in any climate and weather. Stick my choices of seeds into a blend that is a no-nonsense solution to my woes of bug out gardening and I have everything I need to garden successfully in an apocalypse.

I need to eat day one of any kind of disaster and my recognition of the weeds that try to take over my garden every year at home teaches me how to survive anywhere with or without doing any agricultural endeavors myself. This principle, this hard won knowledge that I feel compelled to share

BASIC CURES FOR BASIC AILMENTS

with you is not something new or brilliant, no indeed hunter gathers and country folks have shared this knowledge for centuries one way or another. But modern folks like you and I haven't been exposed to such wisdom and it's as obscure to us as operating a computer would be to a mountain man. There is nothing about it that seems innate or self-explanatory because we don't observe the same signs they did to look to for their survival.

They observed nature, climates seasons and weather and observed what plants and animals were doing all their lives often times. They asked indigenous peoples less advanced in technology or known commercial agricultural practices what was working for them and discovered many new economically viable species as well as heightened survival skills.

It wasn't that long ago that the majority of people here in the U.S. lived on a piece of land where we got at least part of our subsistence out of but yet with all the hunting and agriculture skills evident in the generations of the great depression millions disappeared off the roles of the census of that period by presumably starvation and or malnutrition related diseases.

The knowledge base of home gardening or identifying wild edible plants is no longer a common attribute and if the same economic

BASIC CURES FOR BASIC AILMENTS

calamity happened today the results would be horrendous. Food stamps didn't exist back then and programs like Social Security, minimum wage, Medicare, Medicaid, prenatal nutrition etc. didn't exist either.

Now that we are living in a society where five out of 10 get foodstamps and are dependant on some form of government assistance we get about 1/3 of the folks living in the U.S. or a hundred million people who can't make it on their own now this minute.

Take into account a kind figure of 10% of the population having some mental issues requiring medication, the border line nut jobs we all know not seeking treatment, that the U.S. has more people in some seriously messed up prisons than any country in the world learning how to be nastier than when they went in, add your diabetics, cancer patients or other chronically ill folks and the factor that 60 % of everyone doesn't have more than a weeks worth of food stored and available if they are cut off from the grocery store or the bank and you get at least 200 million zombies that statistically speaking don't know you can eat a dandelion but would be willing to give grass a try if they were starving to death. How many would turn cannabalistic and be willing to give you a try for dinner remains to be seen.

BASIC CURES FOR BASIC AILMENTS

The unknowns and ramifications of a supply chain global famine without outside aid are not well studied but have predictable results. It's bloody chaos that takes about a century to get over if history is an indication before civilization as we know it starts back up again and enough people are still around to write poems and songs that the artists try to reproduce in their renderings of how truly bad things are when we forget how to survive the past calamities and how lowly weeds or animals saw us through these hard times.

Fate is fickle and unrepentant about sorting those folks out that fail to adapt to change but it is much harder on those that fail to remember past lessons in survival.

The old axiom that "Those who fail to remember history are doomed to repeat it" always rings true and those who have no knowledge of the old time wisdom involved in surviving in distant lands or climes will fare no better.

One thing I want you to do daily is watch the alternative media headlines. Know what's going on in the world and your community at many different levels.

We can learn a lot about survival off grid now if we stop to monitor our own newsworthy headlines but most people do not take the time to register or research such facts in evidence. Look at

BASIC CURES FOR BASIC AILMENTS

Syria for example at the date of this writing which has 80% of its people living without power for more than 900 days. Recently as an example to take note of is after Hurricane Irma etc. Puerto Rico will be without power for 6 months!

How about the lessons learned of Bosnia, Herzegovina which was torn apart by civil and religious wars add in the strife and war in the Congo every few years and the constant droughts occurring in Ethiopia and Somalia and begin to see a pattern. Remember Argentine and Venezuela economic collapses.

People live on what they can or have stored and use all of what they know to survive before civilization or aid arrives eventually to gather up the remaining survivors looking for some food security under often times slave like dependence to a new regime.

As long as you can eat something of your own production you still have a choice of acceptance or rejection to emergency or otherwise government policies no matter how bland or bitter tasting your alternative might be!

But as a collective let me explain a history lesson or two about how old Ben Franklin warned us about always remaining vigilant about and remember.

BASIC CURES FOR BASIC AILMENTS

He stated that and I am paraphrasing "Those that give up a little bit of liberty for a little bit of safety deserve neither" and these words echo in my head as the government bureaucracy allows GMO foods, enhanced pesticides, non reproducible vegetable seeds and other franken fish gene splicing type horrors to occur while also trying to control the very liquid of life and outlawing the collection of rain water while allowing an oil fracking crew to pump enough chemical laden water into your environment to cause earthquakes and your tap water in the community to catch on fire in one of those "oops" mistakes that happen and get buried in the media without a whimper from the majority of the unaffected at the moment community.

The Russians were, and still are, a master of controlling those that don't follow the states Pograms and mandates and intentionally starved millions to death in what used to be the breadbasket of Europe for farming wheat and other grain crops while the peasants tried to find enough weeds if they remembered them to survive.

Always remember that food is used as a manipulation and proof of power by government agencies that seek to suppress dissent. Freedom and thoughts of revolution generally speaking come about when the controlled government subsistence to the big corporation or state run cooperatives to live up to the promise of plenty for

BASIC CURES FOR BASIC AILMENTS

the dependant population after years of regrets and strife from moving from an independent or consumer driven economy.

Bread lines, charitable soup lines, etc. follow economic as well as agricultural collapses on a national scale, on a personal scale they can occur as quickly as tomorrow with job loss, homelessness and a variety of other incursions.

Can you find food in the city or the country for yourself with no outside assistance long term? No, most of us unfortunately can't nor most of us would be healthy or resourceful enough already to undertake such a challenge yet we see people attempting it every day whether from need or premonition of something big is going to happen to our food reserves and economy.

The writing is on the wall, charitable food banks are understaffed and have increased demands that are not being met, homeless shelters are already filled to capacity when available, cities try to hide their homeless by busing them else where or creating laws that it is illegal for a private citizen to give them aid or sustenance. It is a tragic and mean spirited world we live in that is only getting worse as the haves and have nots try to distance themselves from each other and human kindness in general.

BASIC CURES FOR BASIC AILMENTS

What if everyone that was homeless knew 13 plants that were edible could be found and eaten and that they didn't have to beg for food or break a law to survive? Would that be a place to start to end a few injustices in this world? Self assurance and reliance in the worst of times that means you can retain your own dignity and resiliency no matter what happens because you have a choice and the knowledge to compound that into something different if you so desired?

Governments and dictators fear this, it removes you from the "system" and it is hard to hold you accountable for anything more than just living by your God given rights to gather food and subsist. You are no longer a tax payer a government education indoctrinated factory worker that punches the man's clock everyday to increase the coffers of the elite and the fascist or statism values they promote to insure their powers over you.

Sanctions, the headlines are alive with sanctions on one country or another of the worst humanity offenders while those that impose them bicker about tariffs and other economic advantages amongst themselves that reflect upon the quality of life its citizens endure. If you could be assured you and your family could eat tomorrow if you didn't get a paycheck this week would you be more apt to layout and sue for regress over unsafe working conditions or wages?

BASIC CURES FOR BASIC AILMENTS

Of course you would if you deemed it truly necessary for a change to occur without already trying to work out your grievances in a chain of command manner without a work stoppage.

Unions got their foothold this way before politicians and crime bosses took over the collective purses the workers created to support strikers and screwed the concept up but the controlling factor of being able to get food to live another day remains. What if we were all working say at a lumber mill and had farms to go home to and being self sufficient food wise wasn't in the cards for the owner to wait the strikers out.

How about the concept that you know you can be dropped off on a street corner or side of the road anywhere and be able to sustain yourself to some degree food wise no matter what? Would this change the way you look at life or prep for the future? Try it for a day or two if you're able, try it just mentally for a moment now without actually having to do it.

Can you find 5 edible plants in 5 minutes that could possibly sustain you today? Would you dare to even conceive of such a thing?

A lot of people think that winter and summer squash has something to do with the best time of planting but that is not true, they can be planted at

BASIC CURES FOR BASIC AILMENTS

anytime. The term refers to storage ability or fresh eating. Some squashes keep longer like Butternut etc. and some are better for fresh eating like yellow squash, zucchini etc. because of their short shelf life.

You should be growing both types. You should also be thinking about where you want to store your excess crop of shelf stable squash and pumpkins because you're going to need to rely on its bounty later. This is where the idea of bug out gardening begins to teach you some staunch lessons in reality.

Now I am going to introduce to you a type of squash called "Seminole Squash" which can last a very long time as a basic staple. (I had one on a kitchen counter for a year and a half and it didn't start rotting until the stem on the end broke off. A paper towel patch on the stem scar added a few months to its continued freshness." Seminole squash is a very old heirloom said to be raised on little island hummocks in the everglades by the Seminole Indians.

They look like little pumpkins growing on very long vines, often the vines get to the length of 30 ft or more. Anyway as they escape your backyard and attempt to go down your driveway you realize they take over a lot of real-estate for a much smaller yield than you would expect.

BASIC CURES FOR BASIC AILMENTS

What to do with whatever is not used or given away is not really a problem because it's only a few extra small pumpkins per vine but they take up space. Thinking about putting in extra vines and ending up say with a months worth if you were forced to eat one every day because that would be all there was soon has you revaluating your planting area and wondering where you're going to put 30 about 9 inch pumpkins. Another squash I like to grow is jumbo pink banana squash; these are a large heirloom variety weighing up to 30 lbs or more. Now add 20 or so of these long squash to your stash and you see we are starting to have a little problem that is if you can grow that much surplus in a season and have added some other food options to get you through winter and the time before next planting and harvest.

The best place to store lots of different kinds of root crops is underground, either leaving them in ground until needed or storing them in a manmade structure like a root cellar. My favorite pretty much self storing and self seeding survival food crop is Jerusalem artichokes which ironically have nothing to do with Jerusalem or artichokes, lots of folks prefer to call them sunchokes by the way. These prolific good tasting tubers are an almost ideal prepper food. However they can take over your regular garden so plant far away.

BASIC CURES FOR BASIC AILMENTS

A pound of sunchokes for planting can be purchased for around $12.00 and could arguably be the best and cheapest prep/food insurance you will ever buy.

The seasons you could possibly be facing of bugging out or remaining bugged in pretty much cannot be chosen or closely anticipated. Yes the credo of preppers is often quoted as preparing for the worst but hoping for the best means you will be most likely stuck at home or in the field in the middle of winter with no chance of planting anything but that doesn't mean there is nothing to do in the garden until spring. There are many tasks you can undertake for preplanting or preparing to stay in your backyard.........

The End

Your Journey To Self Reliance Does indeed start in your own backyard! Explore yours, plant a garden and happy prepping!

Now I am not about trying to reinvent the wheel and this book wouldn't be complete unless I put you in a ready set go mode with the proper attitude. Attitude has everything to do with survival.

BASIC CURES FOR BASIC AILMENTS

I refer again to the Army Survival manual here for the simplest mindset that I can give you that covers everything pretty much. I know I will get detractors for just citing this passage but it doesn't need any editing or additions at this level. This was the way I was taught so it's good enough for you to please consider as is under collective commons license.

This is all based on ARMY FM (Field Manual) that has to do with survival. This manual is based entirely on the keyword SURVIVAL. The letters in this word can help guide you in your actions in any survival situation. Whenever faced with a survival situation, remember the word SURVIVAL.

SURVIVAL ACTIONS

The following paragraphs expand on the meaning of each letter of the word **survival.** Study and remember what each letter signifies because you may some day have to make it work for you.

S -Size Up the Situation

If you are in a combat situation, find a place where you can conceal yourself from the enemy. Remember, security takes priority. Use your senses of hearing, smell, and sight to get a feel for the battlefield. What is the enemy doing? Advancing? Holding in place? Retreating? You will have to

BASIC CURES FOR BASIC AILMENTS

consider what is developing on the battlefield when you make your survival plan.

Size Up Your Surroundings

Determine the pattern of the area. Get a feel for what is going on around you. Every environment, whether forest, jungle, or desert, has a rhythm or pattern. This rhythm or pattern includes animal and bird noises and movements and insect sounds. It may also include enemy traffic and civilian movements.

Size Up Your Physical Condition

The pressure of the battle you were in or the trauma of being in a survival situation may have caused you to overlook wounds you received. Check your wounds and give yourself first aid. Take care to prevent further bodily harm. For instance, in any climate, drink plenty of water to prevent dehydration. If you are in a cold or wet climate, put on additional clothing to prevent hypothermia.

Size Up Your Equipment

Perhaps in the heat of battle, you lost or damaged some of your equipment. Check to see what equipment you have and what condition it is in.

BASIC CURES FOR BASIC AILMENTS

Now that you have sized up your situation, surroundings, physical condition, and equipment, you are ready to make your survival plan. In doing so, keep in mind your basic physical needs–water, food, and shelter.

U -Use All Your Senses, Undue Haste Makes Waste

You may make a wrong move when you react quickly without thinking or planning. That move may result in your capture or death. Don't move just for the sake of taking action. Consider all aspects of your situation (size up your situation) before you make a decision and a move. If you act in haste, you may forget or lose some of your equipment. In your haste you may also become disoriented so that you don't know which way to go. Plan your moves. Be ready to move out quickly without endangering yourself if the enemy is near you. Use all your senses to evaluate the situation. Note sounds and smells. Be sensitive to temperature changes. Be observant.

R -Remember Where You Are

Spot your location on your map and relate it to the surrounding terrain. This is a basic principle that you must always follow. If there are other persons with you, make sure they also know their location. Always know who in your group, vehicle, or aircraft has a map and compass. If that person

BASIC CURES FOR BASIC AILMENTS

is killed, you will have to get the map and compass from him. Pay close attention to where you are and to where you are going. Do not rely on others in the group to keep track of the route. Constantly orient yourself. Always try to determine, as a minimum, how your location relates to–

- The location of enemy units and controlled areas.
- The location of friendly units and controlled areas.
- The location of local water sources (especially important in the desert).
- Areas that will provide good cover and concealment.

This information will allow you to make intelligent decisions when you are in a survival and evasion situation.

V -Vanquish Fear and Panic

The greatest enemies in a combat survival and evasion situation are fear and panic. If uncontrolled, they can destroy your ability to make an intelligent decision. They may cause you to react to your feelings and imagination rather than to your situation. They can drain your energy and thereby cause other negative emotions. Previous survival and evasion training and self-confidence will enable you to vanquish fear and panic.

BASIC CURES FOR BASIC AILMENTS

I -Improvise

In the United States, we have items available for all our needs. Many of these items are cheap to replace when damaged. Our easy come, easy go, easy-to-replace culture makes it unnecessary for us to improvise. This inexperience in improvisation can be an enemy in a survival situation. Learn to improvise. Take a tool designed for a specific purpose and see how many other uses you can make of it.

Learn to use natural objects around you for different needs. An example is using a rock for a hammer. No matter how complete a survival kit you have with you, it will run out or wear out after a while. Your imagination must take over when your kit wears out.

V -Value Living

All of us were born kicking and fighting to live, but we have become used to the soft life. We have become creatures of comfort. We dislike inconveniences and discomforts. What happens when we are faced with a survival situation with its stresses, inconveniences, and discomforts? This is when the will to live- placing a high value on living- is vital. The experience and knowledge you have gained through life and your Army training will have a bearing on your will to live. Stubbornness, a refusal to give in to problems and obstacles that

BASIC CURES FOR BASIC AILMENTS

face you, will give you the mental and physical strength to endure.

A -Act Like the Natives

The natives and animals of a region have adapted to their environment. To get a feel of the area, watch how the people go about their daily routine. When and what do they eat? When, where, and how do they get their food? When and where do they go for water? What time do they usually go to bed and get up? These actions are important to you when you are trying to avoid capture.

Animal life in the area can also give you clues on how to survive. Animals also require food, water, and shelter. By watching them, you can find sources of water and food.

WARNING

Animals cannot serve as an absolute guide to what you can eat and drink. Many animals eat plants that are toxic to humans.

Keep in mind that the reaction of animals can reveal your presence to the enemy.

If in a friendly area, one way you can gain rapport with the natives is to show interest in their tools and how they get food and water. By

BASIC CURES FOR BASIC AILMENTS

studying the people, you learn to respect them, you often make valuable friends, and, most important, you learn how to adapt to their environment and increase your chances of survival.

L -Live by Your Wits, *But for Now,* Learn Basic Skills

Without training in basic skills for surviving and evading on the battlefield, your chances of living through a combat survival and evasion situation are slight.

Learn these basic skills **now**–not when you are headed for or are in the battle. How you decide to equip yourself before deployment will impact on whether or not you survive. You need to know about the environment to which you are going, and you must practice basic skills geared to that environment. For instance, if you are going to a desert, you need to know how to get water in the desert.

Practice basic survival skills during all training programs and exercises. Survival training reduces fear of the unknown and gives you self-confidence. It teaches you to *live by your wits*.

BASIC CURES FOR BASIC AILMENTS

S — Size Up the Situation
(Surroundings, Physical Condition, Equipment)

U — Use All Your Senses,
Undue Haste Makes Waste

R — Remember Where You Are

V — Vanquish Fear and Panic

I — Improvise

V — Value Living

A — Act Like the Natives

L — Live by Your Wits, *But for Now,* Learn Basic Skills

My Readers Might Also Enjoy:

**THE RURAL RANGER A SUBURBAN AND URBAN SURVIVAL MANUAL
&
FIELD GUIDE
OF TRAPS AND SNARES FOR FOOD AND SURVIVAL**

By Ron Foster

The Modern Day Survival Primer for Solving Modern Day Survival Problems! This book will teach you the techniques to not just survive, but to use ingenuity and household items to solve your problems scientifically with a bit of primitive know how thrown in. A complete and detailed section utilizing explicit drawings and easy to understand photographs covers thoroughly the topic of survival trapping using Modern Snares, Deadfalls, Conibear Traps, and Primitive Snares. This book is dedicated for long term survival in the country or the suburbs to insure you survive and thrive! Build a solar oven or pasteurize water, its all in here! Catch your dinner, then cook it or preserve it, too! Food procurement is the name of the game along with purified water in a survival or disaster situation. Are you ready?

The Bug Out Gardening Guide: Growing Survival Garden Food When It Absolutely Matters

What exactly is Bug Out Gardening?
Having your own garden in your own back
yard is great but what if you must evacuate

and have to go to a remote location or start up a garden on a bunch of bad soil? Most Preppers have already realized that besides having dried foods stored foods for a disaster, one can also have fresh grown foods with a little effort supplementing their diets. This book will teach you how simple it can be to take along the materials with you to create a small survival garden. Learn to make your own DIY miracle grow and homemade insecticides and fertilizers! Learn about growing vegetables from scratch when it absolutely matters before you find the stores are all closed and that you lack basic materials.

Envision a portable system of gardening that you can instantly create your homestead with or take along for a long-term bug out situation. Imagine that this system allows you to garden anywhere, compost anywhere and thrive everywhere. Everyone should have access to healthy organic food and this is gardening made easy.

Whether your plan is to bug out or bug in, whether or not you want to start a garden on your balcony or move to the country someday, this is the system for you. Learn gardening tips and tricks along with survival techniques. Plant your very own portable medicinal garden and gain experience with remedies. Learn to grow food in a disaster and feed your family. This and so much more is included in this book. Gain the knowledge of how to create a Bug Out garden that can be assembled anywhere or explore other systems to double your current gardens output and sustainability in a small space. This book includes a Preppers Herbal Guide to medicinal plants and their uses.

The Possum Prepper Guide: How To Buy A Homestead And Thrive During A Disaster

Possum Prepping is different from normal prepping because your focus is on becoming sustainable long term Survivalism with a slant toward self sufficiency. A detailed explanation of using country wisdom along with frugalness and modern technology to be able to adapt and thrive both before and after a disaster. Detailed drawings of traps and snares as well as other food procurement techniques.

The book uses a modern hands on approach of utilizing common household items to enable the average person to actually take a box, a cooking bag and a piece of cordage and be able to feed themselves and purify water.

Check Out The Original Beloved Classic Prepper Trilogy

Preppers Road March

A solar storm has just hit the world causing an EMP event. An emergency manager visiting Atlanta GA must find his way back home after this electromagnetic pulse has stranded him away from his vehicle and his beloved "bug out bag". With 180 miles to go to his destination, David must let his street smarts and survival skills kick in, as food and water becomes scarce and societal breakdown proceeds at an unrelenting pace. An interesting and often funny cast of characters from the Deep South, help the displaced Prepper on his way, as he shares his knowledge of how to make do with common items in order to live another day. Ultimately, he acquires an old tractor and heads for home on a car-littered interstate. This is book one of the Prepper Trilogy.

BUG OUT! Preppers on the move!

Book two of the Prepper trilogy finds the disaster planner and emergency manager Dave faced with the choice of bugging out with his cohort of friends and family, as he watches the societal collapse and demise of civilization around him after an electromagnetic pulse (EMP) solar storm has taken out the grid. A post apocalyptic fiction series that takes you through the trials and tribulations of survival after the predicted NASA 2012 solar super storm unravels the lives and lifestyles of a group of modern day survivalists. The preppers decide on a lake front bug out, with bags in hand, as well as a unique group of operating vehicles from a bobcat loader to a lawn tractor. Will they survive? Could you? Let us find out, and join the party down the desolate dystopian landscape of a new beginning in a world without lights or technology.

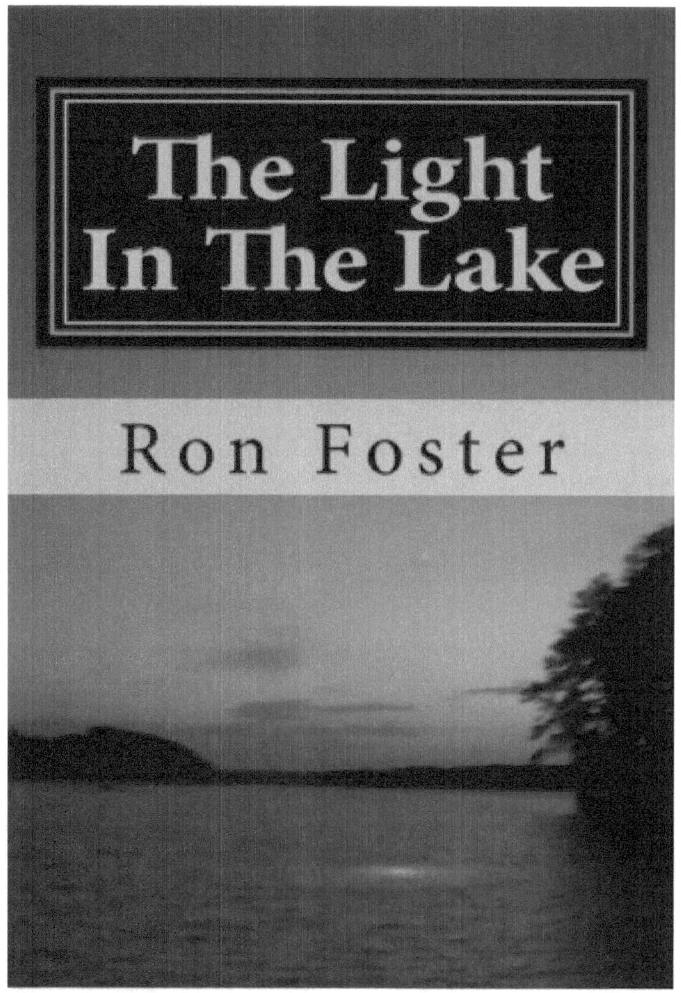

The Light in the Lake

Book three of the Prepper Trilogy finds our band of refugees from a solar storm safely moved into a several lake cabins and trying to work on their short term and long term survival. The lake is a beautiful place for a survival retreat, but is it safe with roving groups of lake residents all looking for what meager food resources remain after a EMP event has shut down society as we know it. Can society be recreated and restarted here, or will starvation and anarchy take over? Can a simple light in the lake be the solution to survival and the reconstruction of society, or is it merely a symbol of what has been and might be yet again?

facing societal breakdown for ten weeks until it is evident he must escape and bug out somewhere. The problem is he only has a half tank of gas and not any means to get any more. His destination requires more fuel than that and he finds himself stuck on the side of a dirt road heading towards a lake cabin he once stayed in. A violent encounter changes his life and his circumstances forever as he tries to protect a boy and his mother in an apocalyptic world. This book is filled with the author's southern prepper fiction humor and wit that teaches you survival skills while entertaining with a tale full of twists and turns.

9 781978 102026